FACING
DEATH

A Conversation with Reverend Bodhi Be

ALAN CLEMENTS

Foreword *by* Mitch Davidowitz, MSW, M.Ed., Ed.S.

Published in 2022 by World Dharma Publications
Copyright © Alan Clements 1997, 2008, 2012, 2020, 2022

Library of Congress Cataloging-in-Publication Data
Clements, Alan 1951 —

Facing Death
A Conversation with Reverend Bodhi Be by Alan Clements

p. cm.
ISBN 978-1-953508-25-6

Death and Dying 2. Consciousness — Meditation — Mindfulness
3. Educational Liberty — freedom — Buddhism 5. Spiritual life —
Buddhism — non-sectarian 6. Human rights — all aspects
7. Social, Political and Environmental justice — all 8. Activism — all
9. Consciousness — all 10. Religions — global 11. Body, Mind & Spirit

First printing, May 29, 2022
ISBN 978-1-953508-25-6

Design and typsetting by Justine Elliott · Design Lasso

World Dharma Publications
www.WorldDharma.com

"There are two ways to live: you can live as if nothing is
a miracle; you can live as if everything is a miracle."

ALBERT EINSTEIN

Foreword

IT IS A GREAT HONOR to write the foreword to this rare and precious book, 'Facing Death' for my beloved friend and dear *Dharma* brother, Alan Clements. I first met Alan forty years ago while I was serving on the staff of the Insight Meditation Society in Massachusetts. At the time he was one of the teachers at the annual three-month retreat, having recently returned from Burma (also known as Myanmar) where he had been living for some years as a Buddhist monk at the Mahasi Sasana Yeiktha Meditation Center, in Yangon. Alan has the unique distinction of having been one of the first Westerners to ordain and train in that ancient (predominantly) Buddhist culture.

Our friendship was both immediate and visceral as I felt the extraordinary presence of Alan's beautiful heart along with his tenacious commitment to truth, compassion and freedom. This was evident in his first book, 'Burma: The Next Killing Fields?' (with a foreword by the Dalai Lama). Alan has gone on to write more than a dozen additional books and films with the same uniquely empowered, nuanced and ethically rooted clarity.

My own work in the area of death, dying and bereavement began with my training as a hospice volunteer in 1978. After my mother died in 1981, I became acutely aware of the lack of understanding around grief and loss. While completing my first postgraduate training in counseling, I published an article with Dr. Robert Myrick titled "Responding to the bereaved: An analysis of 'helping' statements". While serving as the Bereavement Coordinator of a local hospice I developed a program for health care and mental health professionals titled, 'Responding to the Bereaved: Breaking the Myth'. I have presented this training at national and regional conferences around the United States for the past 37 years. In addition to my work as a grief therapist and educator, I utilize my decades-long experience of intensive training in *Vipassana* (Insight) meditation which began in 1974.

For generations, death has been a taboo topic in our culture. In some families, the name of the deceased could not be mentioned. Unlike other cultures where death is honored and celebrated in the light of day, we have often kept it hidden in the darkest of shadows. Doctors viewed death as a failure. Patients were not told of their terminal diagnosis, while others requested that they not be told. Many adults feel resentful that they were not permitted as children to see a beloved grandparent or parent in the hospital prior to their death, or at the funeral. The ability to integrate a death into one's heart and soul is greatly aided by seeing the body of the deceased. The conspiracy of denial surrounding death has deprived those with terminal illnesses and their families of the opportunity to say goodbye. Dying is an extraordinary time to bring the lights of love and forgiveness to relationships that have been challenging or estranged.

The pandemic has certainly raised our awareness of death as we saw trailers storing bodies that morgues could no longer hold. Death has knocked on many doors in sudden and unexpected ways. In this very powerful book, Alan Clements takes this awareness and amplifies it with profound reflections which awaken our understanding. He brings his own experience of being diagnosed with a life threatening heart condition, and the likelihood of dying without an immediate dangerous surgery, to this deep exploration about what truly matters in our own life and death. When Alan asked his dear friend Aung San Suu Kyi (Burma's imprisoned Nobel Peace Prize laureate) "What does your country's 'Revolution of the Spirit' mean?", paraphrasing her answer she replied, "Having the courage to care about things larger than your own self-interest." Alan Clements brings that same treasured commitment to this book as he dialogues about the many seen and unseen deaths on this planet, including the catastrophic realities of climate change and even that of "facing extinction".

Facing Death is both a timely and timeless book (designed to be read in one sitting) that addresses and transcends the questions which focus exclusively on one's own life. As he has done his entire life, Alan seeks a sacred intimacy with a topic that frightens most of us.

To this end, Alan knocks on the door of life and death in a vibrant dialogue with Reverend Bodhi Be, a pioneer in the field of conscious dying and death. He is the Founder of *Doorway Into Light*, a nonprofit educational and charitable organization in Haiku, Hawaii committed to helping others show up for life and death.

I highly recommend this book for anyone who wants to understand this fundamental reality of our lives. It addresses the many threads in the tapestry of a meaningful life and death. It shines light into those dark places that we are often afraid to enter. Alan Clements and Reverend Bodhi Be open a deeply transparent window into our universal struggles with living and dying. Each does this by allowing the raw vulnerability of their hearts to carry the voice of truth in the most illuminating of ways.

Mitch Davidowitz, MSW, M.Ed., Ed.S.

Preface

GREETINGS, DEAR READER. Thank you for being
with me at the beginning of this journey and allowing me to offer a short preface to my book, *Facing
Death: A Conversation with the Reverend Bodhi Be.*

Many of you know this already, but for those
who don't, about a year ago I was diagnosed with
a potentially fatal heart condition. A routine scan,
that discovered only a cracked rib, also revealed an
acutely enlarged aortic aneurysm, an often-lethal
swelling in the largest vessel leaving the heart. I
was told in no uncertain terms that it was like a ra-
diator pipe ready to burst, a ticking time bomb on
a short fuse, and that death could and likely would
come "at any second" if I did not undergo immediate open-heart surgery.

I scheduled three surgeries and cancelled them all due to the shock and the adjustment, the investigation and conversations, and the tears, inevitably, of facing something so dramatic. I decided to come to Maui, my second sacred spiritual home (after Burma) to enter hospice and apply for the right to take my life.

Hawaii is one of the four states in the U.S. that allows the right to die by your own choice, and through a rigorous process I was granted the pharmaceutical substance necessary, should I make this decision. I called it "the rebirthing elixir," and, here in hospice with this elixir, I took care of all the essentials needed to transition, either through biological discontinuity or the fatality of the heart illness and/or consciously choosing my own exit.

I took care of business. I went to see my beloved daughter, Sahra Bella, in Vancouver. I wrote my will and my Five Wishes. I looked deeply into who would handle my burial and my body. Reverend Bodhi Be, here on the island, at his green funeral organization, Doorway Into Light, with its Death Store, had attracted me. I had known of him, and met him, had respect for him, and he agreed to handle my body and bury it, here on the island, whether I die by natural causes or choose to consciously, mindfully euthanize on my most sacred terms.

I've had this vision now for some months, and the only thing that was left was a heart-to-heart with the man that I entrusted, who bequeathed me with his compassion and good will, to take care of my body and bury it, just up the street, should I die here. I felt pressing questions in perhaps a little sharper detail; "Who are you? Who are *we?*" I wanted to get to know him.

This book, *Facing Death*, is perhaps the most sacred conversation I've ever had. It was deliberately designed to be one sitting, to be read in an hour to an hour and a half, to be felt, to be resonated with, to cry along with us. To use the cliché, "No one of us is an island", and we live in a world and time in which death is ever-present, a shadow the limits of which reach into every sphere, known and unknown, more often unacknowledged than acknowledged.

We sit and talk in the context of the Ukrainian/ Russian conflict, and with it the threat of a new world war. Countries are on nuclear alert as a global meltdown unfolds and climate collapse brings with it some of the most biting questions and difficult answers. Even as we speak, multiple extinctions go on in multiple universes and multiple galaxies. Inbuilt into the system, to state the unthinkably obvious, is death.

Within it, we each have our religion, our prayer, our miracle, our hope, our mindfulness, our *Dharma*. This sacred conversation is meant to illuminate, in the humblest way, this epic archetypal issue of life and death. What does it mean to mindfully, consciously inhabit the inevitable? As Bodhi Be says, "We all know we're going to die but we don't know when." It's inbuilt into the system.

This book is part prayer, part scream, part hymn, part meditation; a sonnet, a love song to God, to each of us. It's not meant to teach anything except to inspire our own humble, vulnerable, authentic, dignified way to face the inevitable. So, may I invite you to enter this portal with us, this conversation, an existential human conversation of the heart. I hope there's something beautiful in it for you, as there was for me, and I know the Reverend Bodhi Be.

Alan Clements
Maui, Hawaii

THIS BOOK IS DEDICATED

To the children
in All countries, all over the world.

And equally, to the child that lies
in the heart of every Adult.

And to the almost-born children everywhere,
in All dimensions of our sacred Universe —

Returning into Life at this very moment.

"To change our culture, to change our lives,
requires the transformation of consciousness,
and few things shift consciousness as quickly
as an awareness of death."

— REVEREND BODHI BE

A Conversation with Reverend Bodhi Be

ALAN CLEMENTS: I have the honor of being with the Reverend Bodhi Be, here at his Maui facility — an extraordinary space, a blessed place and so very human and alive, even though it is called The Death Store. It's a center serving the community both as a funeral and burial service, and also a non-profit known as *Doorway Into Light*. I'm looking forward to an intimate and illuminating conversation, exploring the Reverend's many years of experience engaging with the universal phenomena of mortality — of facing death and dying with grace and courage. I'm honored to be in your company, friend.

I've had the blessing of knowing you for some years now, and more intimately these past few months. As you know, I came to Maui after a diagnosis in Los Angeles of a lethal heart disease. At the time, I had not heard of the illness, when the Emergency Room doctor said, "You have an acutely enlarged ascending aortic aneurysm, and unless you undergo immediate open-heart surgery, it's likely to be fatal."

Days later, the Head of Cardiac Surgery at UCLA explained, "The aorta — the largest vessel leaving the heart — will likely rupture at any time. Essentially, you have a ticking time-bomb inside your chest, on a short fuse."

After weeks of follow-up tests and my own investigation, I said 'No' to surgery, as the dangers outweighed the risk, and my desire to live longer was amplified. Then I came to Maui, a well-known haven of mine over the years, to live and die whenever; and to ask you, Sir, that when I pass away, if it's here on Maui, that you kindly care for my body, facilitate its burial, and do so without a memorial. I am grateful that you graciously agreed.

I also came to Maui for hospice care, and after being evaluated as 'Terminal', I was accepted. And further, after due process under Hawaii's existentially elegant 'Our Choice, Our Care' Act (or the Death with Dignity Act) I was given the sacred elixir to mindfully euthanize whenever I choose. It now sits at the base of my Buddha statue in my temple-home, surrounded by other reminders of the Holy.

Without a doubt it's been a challenging time on multiple fronts. Beyond the immediate shock and subsequent gradual integration, I'd never written my will or five wishes, or an advanced directive, and I had certainly never considered what I would want done with my remains. That in itself can take you down, even if you're regularly dosing mind altering substances, meditating, and being in therapy, as I am. So, that's a bit about me.

Now, it's my honor to introduce you, Reverend Bodhi Be, who as a long-time resident of Maui and is the founder and executive director of *Doorway Into Light*, an educational and charitable organization. *Doorway* began in 2006 and operates Hawaii's only non-profit and 'certified green' funeral service. It also operates an educational resource center and store on Maui, appropriately called *The Death Store*.

Doorway Into Light has been offering classes and trainings for fifteen years now, in conscious living and mindful dying, preparing for death, and the conscious care of the dying and the dead. Their Death Doula trainings are attended by professionals and lay people from all around the world.

So, let's dive into this all too human, somewhat surreal topic of facing what all of us are facing (whether we see it or not) along with every other human, animal, bird, fish, insect, planet and tree, indeed every molecule of everything everywhere in the universe, living and disappearing at this very second: our own mortality. Death and Birth. On and on ... The Buddha called it *Samsara*.

Where shall we begin?

REVEREND BODHI BE: Well, you called this place 'extraordinary', and then you said "...and so very human", and of course, the extraordinary is the 'extra' ordinary. It turns out that *Samsara* is precisely where the miracle actually lives, in the 'extra' ordinary. And what's a miracle? It's something that cannot be explained.

When I speak to groups of people, I often ask, "How many of you know you're going to die, and you don't know when?" And I find that everybody raises their hand and looks at me like, 'That was a silly question, everybody knows they're going to die, and they don't know when.'

Now I don't think that's actually true. It turns out that's another piece of information that people have in their heads. Maybe they've seen other people die, but in terms of an embodied, realized truth that people live with in their daily lives, when I look around it doesn't look like that's true at all. Most people seem clueless when living in the truth and reality of 'We're going to die, and we don't know when', and 'Everybody we love and care about is also going to die, and we don't know when'.

That doesn't mean we need to walk on eggshells. But that piece of information may be the most important, commonly known truth there is — that *we're going to die, and we don't know when* — and maybe the least known about. To find a way to live with that truth in beauty, in a holy and sacred way, in a way that actually brings deep benefit, is a powerful practice.

I ask groups, "What's your ideal scenario of a good death?" And if you can believe it, 90 out of 100 say, "I want to die in my sleep." What that tells me is that people, by and large, want to skip the dying part completely. They don't want to participate in their dying; they want to go to bed healthy and happy — and die in their sleep.

21

Most people don't see any value in the dying part; and some of that feeling is understandable. There are many horror stories involving the medicalization and technologizing of death. Most people are dying from diseases that can take years to die from. Few see any value in the actual dying process, the time between getting the diagnosis and death.

AC: Understandably. There's so much perceived suffering projected into the process of dying. Life support. Tubes. Incontinence. Drugs. Yet the denial of death is one thing, and the dismissal of the dying process as having merit is another, right?

And yet one could say, jumping along here — and it is being said — that the whole of the planet and every living being is dying and in hospice today. That is to say, with climate collapse well underway, many say the collapse into extinction is irreversible. That recognition in itself can cause irretrievable despair.

Of course, it would be challenging to find anything beneficial in it, unless perhaps you are a *bodhisattva* dedicated to turning every obstacle, come what may, into wisdom and compassion.

We're also in a pandemic, fear-driven or virus -based or both, where the fear of disease, suffering and death are so prevalent today that they've become daily considerations for many people, worldwide. It is rare to meet anyone who has not been significantly impacted by the virus and its mandates.

My question is: What are some of the key points that you could share with those who are in hospice at this time, who are terminal — in the process of dying and knowing it — to offer support and inspiration enabling them to face their own condition with greater heart, courage and mindfulness?

RBB: [Laughs] In an hour and a half?

AC: [Laughing] Well, let's remember, right, that we're all in hospice, whether we know it, or like it, or not. And time is of the essence. [Laughing] But please, take your time. Death will wait for us to finish our conversation!

RBB: I wouldn't say that we're all in hospice, but I would say the planet is. I heard you say earlier, and again just now, that death is prevalent. Honestly, in my view it's not any more prevalent than it's always been. It's just that there's more awareness around it because there's a pandemic, and now you can die from contact with your friend, or even your family. And as well, there's much more awareness about whether we're going to be the last generations of humans to inhabit this planet, and what that brings up in terms of grief. And yes, 'eco-grief' is very real, and potentially debilitating.

One of *Doorway Into Light's* functions, and a function of *Death Doulas,* is to be a placeholder in the community, reminding us that *death is always present, and has always been present.* Like you said, there is no life without death. Just study the natural world and you'll see that. Yet, death has had lousy marketing over the last couple of hundred years, at least in Western culture. In so many other cultures, especially in the East, death and dying are celebrated and honored as important times for emotional, psychological and spiritual transformation, as well as for immense healing, both personally and communally. Maybe in the West, where we view anti-aging and physical immortality as good ideas, we see death as the ultimate insult to the notion that humans are somehow above — and immune from — the laws of nature.

Coming back to your question, "What do I say to people who are dying?" That depends on how that information is brought to me. Sometimes my response is "Wow." I think it's more of a question of how you face walking towards your own death, and embrace the dying as it is, rather than what I see so much of, which is *people refusing to die while they're dying.*

AC: That's powerful. Please continue.

RBB: And this is so important. In other words, how do we face forward, lean into dying, meet it, befriend it, elevate it with everything good and true? Not just to accept it, but to embrace it. What does that look like to you? And what heart-work needs to be done, to come to a place of completion and contentment with the truth of your imminent, or approaching death? It's in the deal we signed up for. We need to die. A healthy life includes its death. Death, too, is part of the miracle.

I'll share with you something that happened the other day. It's poignant because you came up in this story.

I'm around death and dying pretty much full time — unless I'm mindfully compartmentalizing it that is, [laughing] when I am with my little grandkids, or in the jungle, or with my wife or in my gardens! But death is a 24/7 thing, and that's a calling that has taken hold of me. It's transforming my consciousness, and that's one of the reasons I encourage people, when I teach, to come into the truth and embody the realization — and truly *live it* as much as possible — that *you're going to die, <u>and you don't know when</u>*.

So, it's Thursday night, I'm driving home, going 50 miles an hour on our highway, and I come over a hill. Of course, it's dark, and there's a line of cars on the other side of the road coming towards me. Suddenly there's a car coming! The driver had decided to pass all those other cars in a 'No Passing' zone, and as I come over the hill, the other car's lights are right in my face. Now if that car hadn't had a way to instantly pull in, and if I hadn't been attentive enough to steer quickly to the right, I think I would've died right then and there. And that shook me deeply. "How fascinating!" I thought. "I'm around death and dying all the time, and that really shook me up."

The reason you came up in the story, Alan, is this. I've thought all along that there's no way I know with any certainty that you're going to die before me, even though it looks like your death is more imminent than mine. But who knows, you may cure yourself through your *Dharma* practice, or die of something completely different than the aneurysm rupturing — or die on the operating table if you were to elect to have open heart surgery. Again, all we know is that *we are all going to die, but we don't know when.* Keeping that truth alive is a powerful force of wisdom, courage and grace, I think — and it brings me into more 'full life' living.

AC: I'm with you, Brother, fully. As you're saying, God's a curve-baller, and death could come at the least expected time, to reiterate your point. Whether we subscribe to it or not, we are all living second to second, one breath at a time. And I think you know that I don't claim any special ground here, (no pun intended), knowing that I've got a head start to the grave on everyone else.

RBB: Well, you can claim it; you are in hospice care, and that's some direct level of acknowledgment that this is really happening. There's some major part of you that's come out of denial. Bravo! Many people don't even make that step. In that sense we're not 'all in hospice'.

AC: Thank you. In part it's because the medical pundits I've consulted — the Tom Brady's of open-heart surgery — have declared a state of emergency within my body. "No surgery, die. Surgery, live. Maybe."

Equally, as a spiritually correct Buddhist, I've had a fascination with death from a young age. And once I became a monk in Burma, I saw how the Buddhists were intimately versed in reflecting upon death as a source of liberation. We were trained to mindfully feel every breath — every sensation of the in-breath, and the same with the out-breath — and to stay in mindful awareness, with each new breath, neither wishing to live, nor fearing dying.

But even so, and with frequent visits to burning ghats and charnel grounds and watching too many surgical autopsies to count, in truth I never really took the 'dying any second' thing seriously — or *felt it* on a visceral level.

Years later, sometimes on a sizable dose of LSD or MEO, I did. But still it was always, generally, a hand's distance in front of me. And even further, I often thought about death not in terms of dying, but in terms of rebirth. In that thought, I've got time again after death to live again in another birth, and so on; rebirthing through *Samsara* until enlightenment. Another very Buddhist thing!

But in truth, now that I'm dying and know it [laughing], I was saying the other day how often, when leading retreats, I used the reflection upon death as a motivation to live more fully and more passionately. But again, now that I *really, really* know that I'm dying, and you also know that you are dying, it's not all that compelling to keep death so close to consciousness, or even as a daily reflection.

RBB: With all due respect, no! I'm not dying! That notion that we're all dying, I don't subscribe to that. Not at all. Think about it. You wouldn't visit a new-born baby and say to its mother, "What a beautiful baby, too bad it's already dying." In my view, that's not true. You wouldn't say that, and I find that this actually does a disservice to the community. It turns dying into 'no big deal'. I think it's very harmful for somebody who is actually dying to hear, "What's the big deal, we're all dying." We're *not* all dying.

AC: I hear you. So, let me ask: What does dying actually mean to you?

RBB: If I may, let me rephrase that. What are dying people doing that we're not doing? That's really the question to ask. Because we're not dying. You have a condition that may cause your death. That's not the same as dying. You *may* be dying. You think you're dying because you've qualified to be in hospice based on your doctors' expectations, so you've stepped through a level of denial to say, "Wow, it looks to me like I'm dying." What happens to people when they find out, often from a doctor, that they're dying? If your understanding is that you're dying, what are you doing that I'm not doing?

AC: Interesting. What brought me into meditation (not Buddhism, but meditation), was the visceral urge for radical organic self-examination — and the felt experiential examination of language and meaning. I think you know that death, in a Buddhist culture, is a relative truth, and therefore an existentially accepted illusion. In other words, death is not an ultimate reality.

RBB: I don't know what that means. Please say more. And I do understand the difference between the absolute and relative realities. But I no longer make either one more 'true' or 'real'.

AC: What it means to me is that death, in the way that we often associate it through the filter of culture, doesn't really happen. Because there is no death, really, other than on a moment-to-moment level — conditions arising and passing away, moment to moment. Call it discontinuity, but not death, right?

By analogy for instance, waves moving across the ocean arise and blend back into the sea. But we can't really say waves *die*, when they re-enter the ocean. Waves ripple along the ocean, but there is no one single or same wave moving across the water.

There's only energy moving molecules of water up and down, just like moments of life: arising and passing, rather than living and dying of experience. Or as a fire comes into existence based upon conditions, and when the right conditions cease, the fire ceases. But fire doesn't 'die'. In other words, language and meaning or semantics are everything, right? Relative truths and ultimate truths.

RBB: You know, this reminds me of a funny thing. It was the Dalai Lama's birthday, and there were a bunch of us there, and people were chanting, "Long Live the Dalai Lama!" And I remember thinking, "Why? He's the 14th Dalai Lama. He's had 14 lives already!" It was just a lighthearted thought; I was thinking about everyone inevitably dying. Tibetans are in a uniquely dangerous situation, and he is in a special situation of course. He and his people get taunted daily about his death, and they pray for His long life as we would for our highest spiritual source and protection. I think they are less terrified these days about what will happen, with so much strength and global support, and so many have thrived educationally and otherwise abroad. Their pain of course is what will happen to Tibetans in Tibet, in the chaos. But, yes, there's this attachment to this embodied being remaining

in their body. I no longer say, "We're not the body."
I say, "We're not *just* the body." God inhabits everything and every moment. Why leave out this
precious body we've been given? Here in our funeral home, we sometimes get to really meet someone
after they've died, through their body. The stress
and burdens have left, and there they are...

Sometimes when people say there's no such
thing as death, I absolutely agree — and I work
to live in that truth. It's not a visceral experience
in a realized and embodied sense, but everything
I experience — and I see it all around me, especially studying nature — everything points to the
deathless.

But to say there is no death... I think that's
more denial. I think there is death and there is no
death, and I don't think either one of those is truer
than the other. Everyone will experience this kind
of death: somebody was here yesterday, and is no
longer here today. Here, and not here....

Of course, the other question is: *Can you die
before you die?* In our Sufi lineage, that's right up
there — you practice dying before you die. To me,
those are referring to two different kinds of death.
Just like going into meditation, you lose the sense
of self; or in making love, you sometimes lose the

sense of self. There *are* deaths there. It's good practice for when you're dying time comes. There are certainly deaths when you get laid off from your job. Or suddenly you're 60 or 70 years old, and you can't do this thing you were well known for doing when you were in your 20's or 30's.

There are lots of deaths. Divorce can be felt as a death. So too with rejection and abandonment. The sudden or abrupt end of *anything* can be experienced as a death. Like being ghosted; I've heard people speak of it as a type of death. But in this conversation, we're talking about a very specific death, which in my view is different to every one of those other deaths.

AC: Yes, using language and defining those key code words that we use to inform and define our spirituality — this is what I call the *Dharma* life. I feel that's essential. To state the obvious, because one uses the word 'death' in one tradition doesn't mean another person either understands or subscribes to that definition or meaning. But we often tend to agree without questioning further.

RBB: Yes, language is crucial. Sometimes we think we're all talking about the same thing, but when we put a word or idea, like 'old people' for example, into a circle of people, we each may have a different idea and image of what that is, based on our experiences, understanding and judgements.

AC: Indeed. It's been challenging for me, both as a speaker and spoken word performer, that I am losing my voice, because of the aneurysm and aortic valve malfunction. And from this, I'm seeing how much of my life has been connected to auditory frequency, tonality, on and on... the power of sound and vibration, the musicality of meaning.

But despite the loss, the sacred silence, being in retreat these past months has brought me into a more intimate experience of life and living and being — and to what love means to me as well, on a visceral level, a somatic level. And also, what dying means to me, what planetary collapse means to me personally, what my most sacred relationships mean to me in real time, now — and not in conditioned memory. Everything is in a highly pixilated tragic-sacred psychedelicized beauty. Frankly I have never felt so alive, now that I am dying. And no doubt that too could collapse at any moment.

But overall, that's what the terminal diagnosis or the death reality has become for me. Not a koan or a mantra or riddle to be recited or solved, or even a tab of existential LSD to illuminate the unseen. It's been a heart opener, illuminating non-complacent and intimate co-abiding; 'me' in context. A more transparent self-presence with the whole, if you will.

But I don't know what death actually is, nor do I have any direct experience of it, other than the obvious — momentary cognitive change, perceptual change, and then the more obvious projection of biological discontinuity: 'Me', this skin-draped skeleton, becoming a corpse.

RBB: You're doing the work of preparing for death: Coming to terms with the life we've lived. What is my relationship to myself? Did I live the life I wanted to live? What is my relationship to community? What is my relationship to the planet? What is my relationship to the Holy? Have I contributed to the greater good in some way? How have I lived? Is there a mess I need to clean up? Are there people I need to apologize to, or forgive, or make sure they know I love them? Or do I need to thank them? What's most important? Did I cultivate a living relationship with 'God' that is helping me now that I'm dying?

I say don't wait till you find out you're dying to do this work, it's harder then. This is the deep inner work that leads to living 'fully alive', and to dying well.

Many people come to us at *Doorway Into Light* who want to be more 'on purpose.' Many have worked for 20 or 30 years in some career and now, because of what's happening in the world, and maybe because of their age, they're going, "Wait a minute, I never got to live the passion of my life."

In ancient Greek mythology there's the story of Procrustes — the rogue smith and bandit from Attica. He had a bed, and on the way to Athens you had to pass through his house and get in his bed, and whatever parts didn't fit in the bed would be cut off! You can take the metaphor of going to Athens as, let's say, the Western version of success; we all know that version of success, and many of us have turned away from that story, and realized that that wasn't success. It illustrates the notion that many of us, in order to go for that particular version of success (which many of us did) we had to 'cut off' parts of ourselves: maybe our creative self, or our artistic self, or our imaginative self.

Now many of those people are recognizing that it wasn't the road to success after all, and they're coming back to reclaim those parts they'd lost, or given away. They want to live more on purpose, from the heart, and in some way contribute in a positive way to what's playing out here. How do we plant seeds of love, wonderment and meaning, and purposely endeavor for the welfare of our grandchildren and great grandchildren, whether we have them or not? They're all our grandchildren. And how much more powerful and important that work is, in the light of our children or grandchildren perhaps being the last generations here on Mother Earth.

AC: Your inspiring words, in themselves, are beautiful. And coming back if I may to my own very personal circumstances: on a basic human level, I don't feel any discernible attachment to keep breathing. I've lived my truth so wildly and for so long, that when I really reflected on what's left undone, there was precious little; it wasn't to write another book, or a film, or a live show, or make love, or swim with the dolphins. It was one thing — to see my precious daughter, and to share with the few people that are my intimates the depth of meaning and purpose and love I feel for them, and what they mean to me, and how indispensable they have been to who I am, to my *Dharma* growth. And now that all that has been done — besides entering a silent intensive meditation retreat, which I am now doing to some extent — it's like, "Now what?"

So, I continue to feel into the greater context. I've studied climate change to some extent, and the notion of human-driven extinction; and I (like a lot of other people, such as Paul Ehrlich, Dahr Jamail, and David Suzuki, the great philosopher and environmentalist from Vancouver) feel that we're already in a mass extinction event. In other words, my humble death and desires prior to death are held in context to planetary hospice, and planetary death.

As we know, when the oceans go, humans go. When the Arctic goes, as the President of Finland told Donald Trump, pretty much all life on the planet goes. So, I'm asking myself: How then to go from the individual, to the community, to the whole of the planet and all living beings? And frankly, out further into the cosmos, and beyond.

On that point, I recently read two books by Michio Kaku, the professor of theoretical physics, titled, *The Future of Humanity* and *The God Equation*. In them he refers to galactic extinctions: simultaneous extinctions going on in multiverses at this very moment.

And of course, bringing it closer to home, even our precious sun will eventually become so hot that its flames will engulf our earthly home.

Gone. Leaving no discernible trace, other than an astrophysical vacancy filled with atoms in mystical silence. No Amazon. No Blockchain. No bookstores and retreat centers. No teacher trainings. Gone. Whatever this thing called death is, it's relative and connects somehow to this neutrino-driven numismatic particle process waving throughout infinity. Kaku refers to it as 'string theory' — suggesting tiny strings make up everything, and that the infinite number of their vibrations, like musical notes, account for novelty in our universe. And I'm thinking, "Alan, how do you deal with grieving the death of all living things, the planet, the cosmos and beyond?"

It comes back to what you're saying, and I know you have a lot to say about this: It's not just the grief alone, it's the questions. "Where are you *not* living? What are you *not* doing? Where is your soul's purpose and true sense of meaning?"

In short, it's "What do you want to do with the preciousness of a full breath, apart from just mindfully watching your breath?" It's action-orientated intimacy, perhaps. How well do you express love? Do you have the courage to communicate a love that has never before been expressed? In other words, "Now what? Make haste before death?" What will you *do*? And *when* will you *do* it?

I'll end with a slight disclosure. Now that I am dying [laughs], and finally know it, I have a slight phobia around intimacy. I think that's one of the less obvious reasons why I became a monk and chose celibacy. I must have had some hesitancy around sexuality, around intimacy, around basic human touch — and now that I am dying...

RBB: You can work it out next time! [Laughs]

AC: Oh my, this is turning into a bit of a confessional! [Laughs]. It must be the influence of the corpse in the fridge next to us! [Laughs]. In all seriousness, I want to work it out this time! That's why I'm trying to stay alive! That's another reason why I came to Maui after nearly a year in lockdown in LA — there are so many goddesses here. But now that I'm dying and have been public about it on my podcasts, I can't even get a hyper-spiritualized escort trained in neo-tantra to take Bitcoin! They tell me they can't risk it, nor do they have liability insurance. (Just joking, of course.)

Even when walking on the beach, the only women who smile are the triple-vaxed, fast-fooders who are vaping in from Jersey. Even the turtles on the beach drag up and lower their eyelids and go to sleep. I do find one of my hospice nurses kinda' cute, however — but apparently, they can't cross professional boundaries!

RBB: That's funny. I had a friend who was dying, and he was giving away everything, but he wouldn't give away his red leather pants.

I liked your question, "Now what?" That's the question. That's exactly the question for all of us. What I've seen teaching people over the years about caring for the dying, is that 98 percent of that caring is how fully you can show up and be present to what is. That's shaped by how well you live your life, by fully showing up and taking off the filters of judgements, fears, conditioning — and thinking that you know what's going on. It all comes back to "How do I show up for a world that looks to me like it's dying? How does one show up, and what does showing up even look like?"

If love is the answer, and that's my truth, what does love look like in this moment? And what, if anything, is in the way of the love and compassion showing up? To change the current story — that is, to change the culture — requires a change in consciousness. That's at the heart of my work and calling as a minister. I have not experienced any spiritual practice that shifts consciousness and changes lives as effectively as the awareness of death.

I often hear my great, great, great grandchildren calling me, whether I imagine it or not, saying, "Grandpa, in the midst of the madness, injustice, the horrors playing out in the world, where so much is broken... what were *you* doing?" Even repeating that to you now, I get goosebumps. I live in response to that question. I'm attached to living because I love the seeds I'm planting and the things I'm working on and building. I may not see the fruits of any of it in this life; and it looked to me, on Thursday night, like it was over! But I've really gotten clear that it doesn't matter to me whether I get to see the fruits, or not. Keep planting. Keep building.

AC: Beautiful. Many know that Aung San Suu Kyi, Burma's Nobel Peace Prize laureate and State Councilor, has been imprisoned for well over the past year. She and many of her most intimate colleagues in government are friends, and we also shared the same *Dharma* and meditation teacher, the late Venerable Sayadaw U Pandita. Since February of 2021, the country has been undergoing a mass murder event, a type of genocide of both people and democracy by the evil dictator and his terrorist military.

Back in 1995 and '96, after Aung San Suu Kyi had been released from her first six years of detention, I went into the country semi-underground and we did a book together titled, *Voice of Hope*. Upon meeting her, the very first question I asked was, "You call your country's nonviolent struggle for freedom and democracy a 'revolution of the spirit.' What in essence does that mean?"

Paraphrasing her answer, she replied, "Alan, it means having the courage to care about things larger than your own self-interest. We must have the courage to see the truth of a situation; does it support freedom — or cancel it? Then comes the courage to *feel* the truth. And from feeling it truthfully, we must *act*. To see, feel and courageously act in accordance with the truth is the essence of non-violent revolution."

How easy it's been to disguise my own self-centeredness over the decades of me mindfully meditating upon me. Me on me. Me mindfully observing me being mindful of me, on and on. I'm so mindful of me I've got excessive meditation disorder!

I've mastered, somewhat, me being mindful of me. But what I learned ever so slowly is that I was not particularly aware of others. By this I mean *true contextual awareness of the well-being of others.* Empathy. Compassion. Caring. Giving. A genuine *bodhisattva* spirit. You could call it basic generosity; a spirit dedicated to sharing and caring for others. Aung San Suu Kyi and Burma's revolutionary activists helped to open that door for me.

Moving on. It's not a 'sacred diagnosis' or a 'special recognition' to know that you're dying. I would like to stay alive. Despite only 'being love' I'd also like to be 'in love', an eroticized creative *Dharma*-alive *Ubuntu*. And as I said, I'd also like to have much more time with my beloved daughter. Beyond being my daughter, she's really interesting to hang with. I love her mind and spirit too.

What is most valuable to me is precisely what I think you are saying: it's planting seeds for the about-to-be born. A contribution to the children. A contribution to Life in other and all dimensions of existence. "Stay alive because there's high-*Dharma* value in having lived this long, and now that you've overcome your own self-centeredness to some extent, what will you do with your hands and your heart? How will you give back? How will you work towards a future to believe in?"

I think that's the message I keep hearing in my heart, and from you as well. Towards that goal, I have just finished a children's book titled, *Tonight I Met a Deva, An Angel of Love.* And I am blessed that the Dalai Lama gave it a beautiful endorsement.

RBB: Wonderful. As for me, I've extinguished the notion that there's such a thing as 'selfish' and 'selfless.' In other words, I've dedicated my life completely to service, and I love how that makes me feel. I do this service work primarily because I see that it's my responsibility as a child of God, and because I am given so much — we're all given enormous amounts that we forget about completely. So much had to happen and is happening for us to be here. Look how much our ancestors had to do for us to be here! I mean, the whole universe is supporting us. The way the earth itself is nourishing and supporting us, I'll never be able to give back as much as has been given to me, or to any of us. In that recognition, that's what I want to do: I want to give back as much as I can. And, awakened consciousness wants to be shared. But if it felt rotten, it would be hard to do that. It feels good to me: in fact, it makes me love my life.

AC: Take your Buddha statues down and put his heart and spirit up there on the wall!

RBB: Just make your selfishness about something bigger than you and your little scene. Make it bigger than your family and your pets and your car, or whatever it is. There is no 'self' anyway; that's a core Buddhist teaching, as you expressed earlier.

We get stuck in the sense of self. And, hey, I love that we're individuals. In my view, God wants to experience and create beauty, and in order to experience so much, it needs all of us, in all the myriad ways we view the world and in all the ways we find ways to create beauty. Humans are amazing in the many ways we create beauty. I love it that there's so many of us, and we're all so different, and too, there's only one of us.

Coming back to your question, "What do I say to people who are dying?" I feel for people who are dying and struggling. I myself don't put much into this idea of 'Rest in Peace' (RIP). Some of us may be reassigned pretty quickly. We're needed. But I do put a lot of attention towards helping people 'Leave in Peace' (LIP). That's what 'dying well' is about.

And as people caring for a loved one and as death doulas, how do we support that? Doing your dying can be hard work, and that can appear as suffering. And for the most part, we don't see any value in suffering. It's at the core of Buddha's teaching as you know, yet. Some of the most important times in our lives that helped us find out who we are and helped build our character were times when we suffered. Sometimes suffering *is* the medicine.

Often the person dying wants more time. That's the most common thing you hear from people when they find out they're dying, "I want more time, I'll do anything for more time." And if you're willing to do anything for more time, often times, more time doesn't look like the 'more time' you imagined. It often means more time spent going to doctors for treatments and medications. But almost everyone wants more time. There's always that next hook: "Boy, I'd love to see my grandchildren grow up. Oh, man, I'd love to see my granddaughters get married. Oh, man, I'd love to have great grandchildren. I still want to see, go, achieve...." The dying have endless reasons for wanting 'more time'! Sometimes the other side of a long-term dying is "How much longer will this take, when will it be over?" Again, it comes back to time.

AC: Beautifully said. Would it be wise for people to make a list of things they'd like to elevate to the status of 'do' rather than 'dream' — or even fear doing — because it may feel so good?

RBB: Personally, I don't believe in a bucket list. Not at all. A bucket list is again a sense of having more time. What do you need to do to be ready to die? Read the book, *A Year to Live*. In the meantime, live the story, *We're Going to Die, and We Don't Know When*. See what comes out of that. See what it is that you're doing now that you need to change about your life, so that you are prepared to show up when it's your turn. Just like you said, who do you need to go back to? When you know *you're going to die and don't know when* as a realized and embodied truth, it'll be less of a surprise when you find out you're dying. Meanwhile, it'll change your life.

We all have a trail behind us, and that trail is either filled with love and respect and gratitude and good feelings and great relationships, or there's potholes on that trail of resentments, anger, lack of forgiveness, unresolved relationships. We all know what those are. Those things show up when you're dying and you're on your death bed. How often does somebody say, "Oh, I need to talk to my son. He's six thousand miles away. Please, you gotta' fly him in right now!" And maybe the son will come, and maybe the son shows up in time, and maybe the son doesn't show up in time, or maybe the son doesn't want to show up at all.

Regarding what we spoke about in the work about completing a life, I don't believe in a Judgment Day, but I certainly see 'self-judgment day.' I so often see dying people who want to be forgiven. And these are not horrible people. These are not murderers. These are good people, and it's because shame and judgment and self-loathing are so prevalent in our culture.

AC: In my experience, you've got to make the altar of your redemption in your own soul. You can't ask other people to give you the gift you need to give yourself.

RBB: Well, in my reality, God is the all-forgiving God. So if we want forgiveness — and again I see so many people that do — we must *want* to let go of shame and self-judgment. And also we must be willing to ask forgiveness from, and forgive, those we need to — whether they're still alive or not.

AC: If I may, a point on forgiveness, quite personal to me. I was brought up as a mystical Christian, my grandparents on my mom's side came to America in 1919 from Syria. And perhaps it was also the influence of psychedelics throughout my youth as well, but I became the President of the Young Christians' Society in my final year of high school in Virginia. By way of saying I loved the life of Jesus and read the Bible quite a bit. One of my favorite passages on forgiveness in real-time — not that I'm particularly good with it — is in Matthew 18:21-22 in the Parable of the Unmerciful Servant. There it says, 'Peter came to Jesus and asked, "Lord, how many times shall I forgive my brother or sister who sins against me? Up to seven times?" And Jesus answered, "I tell you, not seven times, but seventy-seven times." I bring that up, as a reminder of the need to redeem oneself through incessant self-forgiveness.

RBB: Amen.

AC: Now moving along into another facet of the living into dying into the rebirthing spectrum. Another prominent element of what I've discovered these past few months is the proactive side of self-forgiveness or self-love: the gift of simplicity, the gift of boundaries, the gift of self-respect, the gift of taking sacred care of your hour, your month, your everything. *How well* do you eat — not just *what*. To walk the first step, breathe the air, see the rainbow, walk into the light... let it fill your being.

It has taken a lot to get here. This has been hard for me over the years. I think I've been conditioned by some sense of scarcity mixed with shame to feel pure joy, transient as it may be.

RBB: We all are. I'm right with you. We've been sold the idea that we won't be happy or content until we buy this, or go there, or collect this, or achieve that, or become something or other. We've been horribly conditioned, and programmed, a good part by TV, that we're not good enough. I heard that the Dalai Lama said something about this when he first came here. That's what he saw right away, this sense of shame and lack, and he was shocked by it. We westerners, who appear to have everything, were suffering.

AC: Yes, the fog of shame. The invisibility of it, so much of the time. It's like a contaminated oxygen; something's off, not quite right. One of the most challenging things I've been feeling is not 'inadequacy' but a hesitation in asking for help, and a reluctance to even express need. I've reflected upon this, many times.

My father was put in a foster home by his dad when he was seven, after his mom passed away. Dad spoke with me at times about how difficult the next nine years were; the abuse and degradation and forced labor. At 16 he lied about his age and joined the Navy and went to war. I think a lot of my hesitation in not asking for something, even more noticeable 'now that I am dying', comes from that influence. A traumatized father subjected to an abusive boarding school joins the military to fight a war. Another reason why I felt so at home as a Buddhist monk in Burma, living in silence with no belongings, and under a dictatorship, no less!

RBB: Yes, tracing the conditioning is revealing. It's a cultural thing too — it's bigger than the home front alone.

AC: Right. So it comes back to how well can you take care of your day. I'm blessed by Matthew Marshall and his partner Griff Griffiths, who are providing me with a humble home-temple, and I've anointed the space with my own aesthetic. I ask myself throughout the day, "How well do I authenticate what's beautiful about this hour?" It's slowed me down. It has quietened my spirit, taken the forward-movement out of living. I'm more monastic today, more meditative today than I was even as a monk. Perhaps I am simply more mature, more evolved. But if I were to say why, I'd say that the lens of *Dharma* beauty is finely polished, and I'm living into something more sublime and larger than dying.

I would encourage people — if they were connected to what I'm saying, or what you are saying — to state something so obvious and yet so easily neglected: slow down, feel, breathe, abide. Be. Beautify your home, beautify your face, beautify your body, beautify your... everything. Be the 'holiness' you admire in the Dalai Lama. How well do you wash your hands? How well do you brush your hair? How well do you bathe? How well do you put cream on your face? How well do you tell your partner you love her? How deeply do you *feel*?

As a meditator, for instance, in the beginning I thought that true meditation started only when I sat down, closed my eyes, and focused inward on the sensations of breathing. But as I learned as a monk and have kept dear to my heart over the decades — and even more so now — is that there's an entire universe of events in approaching the cushion that are equally as elegant and potentially illuminating as finally sitting still.

In other words, anointing the day with tiny acts of grace is one of the greatest gifts that one can give oneself. Don't wait for a diagnosis, or reflection that you're dying, or being with people who are dying. Slow down, feel; expand into the nuances of the moment flowing forward — and perhaps backward, simultaneously. After all, we are in a directionless infinity in life.

But coming back to 'where the rubber meets the road', so to speak: One of the hardest things for me these days is driving. Since the aneurysm can rupture at any time, and with no warning, I don't want to crash and harm anyone. And my doctors have told me many times, with no intention to scare me, that a rupture could (and will) happen, without more than a few seconds warning, at any time. It's a dilemma.

RBB: In America an average of 400 people die every day in an accident. In other words, 400 people who were doing all the right things, good people giving their time and money, will die today in an accident. And tomorrow, 400 more people who went to bed happy and content will wake up and die, on average.

Of course, we're so filled with factoids and overloaded with information that this doesn't touch us. We think "Oh, that's not *us*, that's *other* people." Well folks, I hate to break it to you — I've spoken to other people, and they don't think it's them either. So, who are these 400 people dying every day?

What you encourage people to do, and people have probably heard this in a million different ways, is this: I heard that one Tibetan Rinpoche said that in the West, everybody's so busy doing all the important stuff that they never get to the *really* important stuff. It's what he called 'Western laziness.' That's a fascinating statement because that's what we see. That's what we all act out a lot of the time. We tend to be leaning forwards. You say, "Come back here, take a bath, make yourself beautiful, say 'Hi' to your feet," for example. "Thank you, toes." But so often we're in this leaning forward thing, focused on what's next, what's next, what's next.

Some of that is actually the fear (and terror) of stopping and noticing how you *actually* feel. Maybe you don't love your job. Maybe you don't love your relationship. Maybe you don't love yourself. Shame and guilt are different, right? Guilt is 'I did something bad'. Shame is 'I am a bad person'.

On top of that there's this low-level anxiety, especially in these current times; we want to hold on to a sense that everything's going to be ok, that we know what's happening, that we're in control. We expend a tremendous amount of energy holding on.

That unwillingness to stop and actually *feel all the way* into what's going on manifests as either leaning forward, being somewhat frozen, or living in the rear-view mirror and feeling that we're victims of what happened. Of course, that was the big message from Ram Dass: "Stop. Be Here Now." THIS is where it's happening. THIS is where love happens. THIS is where God happens. THIS is where death happens, and THIS is where life happens, and this beautiful thing called The Dance of Life and Death.

If you study nature, if you spend time in nature (and I do), you see that there's this amazing dance happening. If you have a garden, you can see that dance. Compost and micro-organisms and bugs and worms are what makes the whole thing work. Everything you eat, no matter what your diet, is nourished and fed by what has died in the earth. It's everywhere. That's what I meant when I said I don't think death is any more prevalent now. There's just more awareness of it now, and it's this beautiful dance. And in the last couple of hundred years it's had lousy marketing, especially in the last 70 years when we've medicalized and institutionalized and technologized dying and death. Dying is not just a 'medical event'. For one thing, dying is a verb, so it's something you *do* or *refuse to do* and then *it happens to you*. It's also what I call an emotional and psychological unfolding, and a spiritual unfolding. How do we get to loving the truth of our eventual death, of loving impermanence itself?

AC: As you're saying, death is everywhere and life itself emerges from the soil of death. My question, Reverend, is this: How does one integrate coming to terms with one's own mortality with planetary collapse, with extinction itself? And before you answer please let me frame the question further: An August 2010 report from the UN Planetary Program stated that 150 to 200 species a day are becoming extinct. Plants, insects, fish, mammals: there it is, as you're saying, right before our eyes... but still so unrecognized. We humans are a coexisting species, in a mutually dependent or interdependent world.

Going further, we now have the concept, perhaps you know it, of 'co-extinction', meaning that if a particular set of conditions collapse, we humans could not sustain. If the oceans go, that is to say if acidification causes the mass extinction of marine life, we risk ecological collapse because the oceans produce half the oxygen we breathe. So as consumerism goes, if the oceans go, then homo sapiens go too. We're having this colossal slow-motion extinction event, every day, every minute, right before our blind open eyes!

Of course, more and more young people are aware of that, like the young Swede, Greta Thunberg, who excoriated world leaders in 2019 at the United Nations for their betrayal of young people through their inertia over the climate crisis. I wrote about the collapse in a dark satirical novel last year titled, *Extinction X-rated.* And today I can hear millions of young people shouting: "Listen, we're suffering from grief and depression knowing we're all going to die. Please take care of the environment. STOP your fetish for stuff. STOP consumerism. STOP your endless wars. STOP your addiction to money, denial and death."

If I may, how would you address that issue? More specifically, what would you say to Greta if she were in the room with us right now? Not only her, but if all the children in the world were listening, what would you say?

RBB: In this moment, I would say we have to grieve. We have to fully grieve and acknowledge all of those feelings around what that looks like and what that feels like. We have to call out what we see is happening. We have to collectively come together and grieve: not talk about our grief, but to give our heart a voice. I've been leading grief rituals in support of that for many years. We must come together, in groups, and grieve out loud. I now see love and grief as twin sisters. I have witnessed so much beauty and power emerge in people who have given themselves permission to grieve, unabashedly, unselfconsciously and unrehearsed.

If we are paying attention, how could we not be feeling deeply about what we're seeing out there, everywhere in the world? I cry for the children. I cry for my grandchildren. I cry for the animals. I cry for the earth. I cry for the countless animals and insects and birds and sea creatures who are gone or are on the run. I cry because of my love of life and all I care about. And we won't see the worst of it; they will though, the children and grandchildren will. And we're all a part of it. If you have a car, a computer, a phone — they're mining in the Congo and putting a lot of those people, even children, to work to get these precious metals that go into our phones, our cars, and computers. All at a price. A big price. And we participate in it every day. We're caught in the whole thing. As consumers and users, even recording our conversations right now, we are all caught in a cycle of collective denigration. And we must grieve that too, that we participate in it.

And what do we love? We love the people and things and places we care about, and we care about the things we love. Sometimes I facilitate wedding ceremonies, and if it's appropriate I'll say, "Look, you're signing up to spend the rest of your lives together; that means you're signing up to one of you being there when your partner dies. That's in the arrangement." That's implicit in the deal of this whole... whatever you want to call it.

Now, I don't call it an illusion. Whatever you want to call it, it's just built in that people you love today you're going to say goodbye to. Or they're going to say goodbye to you. Love and grief are twin sisters, whether it be personal, or global, or interdimensional.

And what would I say to dear Greta? First of all, "Thank you, Greta. Thank you, from my heart. I wish every young adult would participate in doing what you're doing in bringing such an awareness to the world, to be such a conscience of our world. I bow to you and all other young people worldwide, for being so aware and so willing to have so much courage and strength and fortitude to do what you do." She and others should be out enjoying life with their friends. What a great time of life that is, and I hope she gets to do some of it. I can only imagine what young people looking around must think and feel about their future and the future of life on earth.

I'd also say that some of us older people *got it* when we were young. In 1970, I saw what was happening, and I realized that if it continued the way it was going, it would look like it does today. I dropped out of college and went to live in the woods in a commune, learned how to live with no electricity, learned how to live with people and grow food and build stuff. It changed my life completely, and I've been on that track for the last 50 years. Not everybody did that. Not everyone at Woodstock did that.

But we all had the opportunity in the 70's, even before there was such a thing as Earth Day, to see what was happening and had been happening, if we were willing to step out of the 1950's TV shows that were conditioning us to think that technology was the key to a beautiful life and never having to work. Now you see that people that don't get to work get to stand in unemployment lines... and just look at what's happening with the homeless!

So, coming back to Greta, I'd also say to her that some of us *really got it* back then, and have been out there working our butts off for the last 50 years. And even so, we cry with you, Greta. We cry with you ... we cry with all the children.

AC: We cry with you, indeed. And yet (or still) everyone's got their foot on the gas pedal of denial, including me, including us.

David Suzuki used the analogy of us humans speeding in a car arguing about what's on the radio as we go headlong into the brick wall of planetary self-annihilation: extinction. Of course, it's a denial fortified with greed and ignorance, and all too often a lot of magical thinking and spiritual lingo!

It brings up the question again: "My God, how do we deal with mortality on an individual and family level, with planetary loss, where maybe all life goes extinct?" And it circles back to "How do we break from the etiquette of grief into compassionate action that supports Greta's generation, my daughter's generation, your children's generation, your grandchildren's generation, and the future of life? How do we break out of grief and the coma of conformity, into caring action?"

And one last thing, (and I know this is an existential conundrum as Michio Kaku states), is that no matter what we do in looking at how to take life off this planet and move it onto other planets, or into other regions of the cosmos, or perhaps through a worm hole into other dimensions, the sun — that keeps us warm and grows all our food — will eventually become so hot it will sterilize our precious planet. And — as I said before — in several billion years, Earth will be vaporized, as in... gone.

How do we come out of grief and denial and actualize caring actions within that larger set of contexts? I know it's a big question, but in the spirit of embracing death and service to the future of life, please if you would, walk us through *A Doorway into Light,* as best as possible.

RBB: It is a big question. But let me give it a go. First of all, I personally don't subscribe to the idea that you 'come out of' grief. I'm not big on the word 'grief' because I don't resonate with the sound of it. It sounds like a stuck place. But *grieving*, again if you see it as the twin sister of love, is something that you carry as a precious gift.

AC: Is grief sadness?

RBB: No. It may include sadness. It's like trying to define love. Would you say love is one emotion? Or would you say love encompasses many emotions that you may be able to enunciate. When you ask, "So give me another word for grief", the answer is 'No'. It's like love. It's this vast thing. It's similar to why a wife says, "Oh, my husband's not grieving" because maybe she has a notion of what grieving looks like, and he's not grieving like her. People grieve in all kinds of ways.

AC: Humanizing attachment?

RBB: I'm not sure where to go with that. Again, people hear the word 'attachment' in very different ways, sometimes as a negative thing. I don't experience attachment as a negative thing, but there needs to be big awareness around the attachment so that our 'clinging' doesn't cause harm to self or others. That's what's happening now: our attachment to our bodies, our attachment to our lives, our attachment to things going along the way we want them to.

What do Buddhists talk about all the time? Impermanence. Sometimes I think God imper-manence. God is embedded in this moment-to-moment, changing universe. There is no 'Be here now' because there is no 'now'. It's impermanent. And we don't get any kind of train-ing in school about impermanence and how to meet change. And yet change is all there is, and we have not had any training in it.

AC: I so agree. I don't think there could ever be enough said about impermanence or *annica* as it is known in Buddhism. Let's pause, allow me to change trajectories.

Over the past few years and more regularly this past half year on island, I've been, as mentioned before, dosing — experimenting with a range of psychedelics, in various amounts and combina-tions, and in a range of settings as well. I've asked myself on a fairly frequent basis (a type of thought experiment or better yet, a psychedelically en-hanced meditative thought experiment) what's missing right now from me realizing the ever-pres-ent reality of *annica*? In other words, if I had a full and radical awakening to the ever-present im-permanence of everything right now, would I be dancing like a rainbow on the beach at Baldwin on the photons of existence, beyond death and dying and grieving?

The Buddha's teachings incessantly point the mind back to that realization: Change is the only constant. If I knew that on the most visceral level, there'd be no issue. Just life, like a rainbow, a spectrum of colors, without inherent 'rainbow-ness'. Conditions in the sky of consciousness, without centrality. So then I ask myself, "Who's grieving? Why am I afraid? And of what?" because I'm not embodying what you just said so beautifully: The felt experience of impermanence as anything other than a set of interrelated conditions without centrality, or some separate 'one' experiencing change.

In my wildest fantasies, I wish we had a psyche-delicized, trans-religious, post-*Dharma* wisdom, that one could breathe in, or dissolve under the tongue, that delivered the full wisdom of imperma-nence — and with it the instantaneous liberation from greed, ignorance and fear. I'm not tripping now, by the way! [Laughing] But I am dying... not really. [Laughing]

Anyway, thanks for hanging with me here and helping me get closer to living and dying.

RBB: [Laughing] We can know just that. Einstein once said, "There are two ways to live your life. One is as though nothing is a miracle. The other is as though everything is a miracle." What I love about that is that it's a *choice*. You can choose to live within life as a miracle, and co-create within the miracle, and expand the novelty of the miracle, so to speak, as God's eyes on the scene.

Of course, the miracle thing often shows up when people are dying. "I want the miracle. I don't want to die." And people will go to the ends of the earth to get a magical miracle cure or a blessing from a holy person, so as not to die. And hey, I don't know what I'll do when it's my turn... Is death part of the miracle?

Back to your own chosen *sadhana*: As I hear you, I must say I have mixed feelings about the psychedelic thing. Don't get me wrong, I've certainly psychedelicized many times; and will likely be a guide for those dying who take this medicine. Now there's an entire movement around psychedelics when you're dying, I get that. I get how psychedelics can be really supportive for anxiety and fear and to help someone 'let go' into their dying and into the healing and opening that wants to happen; and too, the real possibility of making contact with what 'doesn't die'. In a way, it's the 'sudden school.'

But I would ask, "Why isn't life psychedelic enough?" It's an amazing miracle that it's even happening, that we're even sitting here. Talking. Breathing the same air. Learning from one another through a shared vocabulary, like strings of auditory musicality and meaning in the context of earth and infinity, and life and loving, simultaneously. It's a miracle, for God's sake! And, it is also simultaneously tempered by birth and death, and extinction and grieving.

But we think we need to take something *more* to illuminate it, enhance it, flow with it, on and on. Of course, that's part of the conditioning. We've been taking pills for everything, so why not take a pill for when you're dying? It's not hard to imagine, given how few people want to do 'the dying part', that dying could become something you simply take a pill for. Imagine designer drugs for dying! As you know, there's a major push for legalizing psilocybin to assist the dying in a number of states now. I can imagine how big a hand government and Big Pharma will have in that!

Anyway, back to your question. The answer to that is that we've become lethargic and conditioned by a culture that tells us God is somewhere else, that there's something wrong with us and this is not our home. And also, we think we have lots of time, so there's a filter between the psychedelic miracle happening in this moment, and how we experience or don't experience that very thing as a way of life.

What's in the way of that? That's the central question. *What's in the way of being fully awake and alive and liberated, within the miracle?*

I thought Ram Dass made a powerful point when he said that he realized he didn't 'come down' from a psychedelic trip, he 'climbed down'.... meaning it was something *he* did, not something that *happened to* him. How many of us were tripping all day and came home to a pile of dirty dishes or some such thing and immediately 'came down.' Obviously, the dishes didn't do anything.

Personally, I don't concern myself with whether there's life after death. I'm more concerned with: "Was there life before death, and what did that look like? And what does that look like for me, right now?"

Again, we come back to, "Am I, are you, showing up fully today?" So fully that you come over a hill and a car's coming right at you, you're there; and a lot of your life to that point has been right there; and when you're standing in front of someone, you're right there as if it may be the last time you see this person.

I personally think *'Knowing, as an embodied truth, that you're going to die, and you don't know when'* is the most powerful spiritual practice I've come across.

It is central to my existence, and I have been teaching it as such for forty years. Before that, I looked around for "Where's the juice? Which spiritual path has the truth? What is this thing about God?" Turns out the miracle is right here, with you and me, in the extra ordinary.

But we tend to get entrapped or side-tracked with these notions of what's really spiritual, and a lot of people think that if you were more spiritually evolved, you wouldn't feel sad or sorrowful in your grief, or you wouldn't be crying over so and so. I think that's such nonsense, and at the same time that thinking kind of makes me cry. Because such people are missing out on so much life, so many beautiful dimensions of being.

Our humanness is deeply spiritual. It is the full spectrum. People often say, "Well, that's just the body." Well, wait a minute, please! If we are the entire universe, why aren't we this too? Why isn't this moment now — whatever it is — as spiritual as everything else? When I guide a circle and offer a prayer, I ask that we invoke the presence of God. Again, 'God' is a placeholder for something beyond any one word. In 'invoking', that is in 'calling in', it's not about calling God to come be with us. What 'invoking' is for me is inviting all of us to call ourselves, our consciousness, into this place where 'God' already is, and that we step into the presence of the Holy.

Yes, I see that something leaves the body upon death; some essence, some spiritual thing. But I don't know that there's an actual thing called 'soul'. And I don't know why there would be. You referred to this earlier, from your Buddhist training. I've heard it described as a portion of the entirety, some constellation of causal conditions. In other words, it's the whole thing and it's also a piece of the whole thing. And consciousness, this matrix of being — call it what you wish — is not anywhere in one part of your body. It's emanating through what scientists now think is the mitochondria; that's where the engine is for the whole thing, in every one of the billions of cells in our bodies. Again, that's what scientists do; they try to explain it.

Of course, it's the snake chasing its tail. And that's the Great Mystery that we're not supposed to solve, and won't — although we'll try. I love that. Sometimes my name for God is 'The Great Mystery'. Not like the Sherlock Holmes mystery where sooner or later you know 'who done it', but the Great Mystery that you live inside of, inside of a big "Wow." It's not really a question. Or is it a question? "Wow, I have no idea what's going on." Most of us are control freaks, whether we recognize it or not. We want to know what's going on. We want to think we know what's happening. The quest to know our origins, our futures, our self, our sub selves, the cosmos, the mind of God: The mystery as miracle. 'I don't know' is actually a powerful place to stand.

AC: Beautiful! I like your God! [Laughing] Going back to a favorite midwife of mine — psychedelics. Listening to you, feeling you and me together as I'm thinking and listening to you, while listening to me interpret you, is as close to life as I can get.

Presence for me, with the other, has been intimately connected to meditation and silent retreats, or what I'd call today here on Maui, the psychedelic of oxygen as an awareness of consciousness to explore the miracle of life. Thanks to you, Reverend Sir! [Laughing] And now that I have chosen to be in retreat again, I've made living life my monastery, and expanded the awareness to a more holistic experience of light and breath and sight and sound and sensation, as a daily meditative practice. And more specifically, when walking alone and barefoot in nature, primarily at my adopted forest sanctuary near Baby Beach, which I've named Deer Park, after where the Buddha was said to have shared his first *Dharma* teaching, near Benares in India. Walking this park for five or so miles a day has changed my life, and to amplify things I often walk after dosing. Among many realizations, it has 'taken the death out of dying' so to speak, and largely removed any concern about 'when'. As you've said, "We don't know when."

Personally, dosing with psychedelics and walking and sitting in nature, essentially naked other than my shorts, is about as empowering and healing as anything I have ever known. Overall, I'd say "Get out of the therapist's office. Get out from within the four walls of whatever. Get out of attending yet another retreat and listening to someone else share their meditative ordeals and listen to your heart and mind and body communing with the trees, flowers, birds, wind and light."

I dare say it, but I will because it is true: It's taken the diagnosis of a life-threatening illness past the medically sanctioned 'cure' of open-heart surgery, to hospice and the drugs to take my own life, to truly start living again, as in really going for it. I think that is what I hear you emphasizing: Live. Live fully.

So here I am in this conversation, feeling great joy again — that's what I'm trying to point to. You talk about mystery, and I'm so into the mystery, and equally the navigation of the adventure.

As I said, I grew up in a military family and we lived in a 32-foot-long trailer that Dad hauled up and down the East Coast and parked on multiple military bases for a year or two, and then onward. From there I attended the University of Virginia until I became sickened by the 'Big American Lie' I was being fed and quit, despite being on full scholarship, and listened against all odds to my instinct for freedom. And I ended up as a Buddhist monk, one of the first in America, in an ancient culture in Burma — where I was blessed to find home, and what felt like the reunion with my true family.

I feel empowered when I reflect on this. "Alan, you went from here to there, by listening to your heart, as hard as that was so much of the time. You navigated an undiagnosed traumatic brain injury, and opioid, alcohol, nicotine and cocaine addiction. You wrote books, you led retreats, you've performed *Spiritually Incorrect* on stages in many countries, you've done lots of things that defied the gravity of your fear, your apprehensions — and your conditioning."

Right now, although I've got this encasement that's going to collapse pretty soon (who knows when), the adventure is ever-present when I'm dosing, or I'm walking, or I'm in communication with intimates, really there. And I go, "Wow, this is really wild, this is really crazy." Just as it is right now, with you.

And yet, furthering this process, I make an about-face and see how it could get really bad; like I could be in Yemen or Syria and starving and traumatized. Or I could be in Burma, compelled to take up weapons and fight the dictatorship, or be caught and tortured (as so many friends have been) and thrown in a gulag to rot and starve to death, alone.

But circling back around, I've been gifted — right here and now — with this extraordinary condition. I often say, "Fuck dying!" You are never more empowered than at this very moment and as you said about Einstein, "Either it's a miracle or not, and the choice is ours."

But what I am really trying to say is, it is beyond me to make a miracle out of rape or torture or genocide or biological war. So then I say to myself, "OK, rise up, take it higher. Increase the dose. Meditate a little bit more, do some more yoga, dance a little bit." I look in the mirror: "Where are you *not*? Where do you want to adventure to, in this life or the next life?" But it is so incomprehensible to put myself in the mind and body of someone acutely suffering.

This brings me to the issue of a next life and re-birth. This is one of the reasons why I did a retreat over New Year, called *Rebirthing into The Future*. It's a new way of looking at meditation and spirituality, and the navigation of this 'thingness' to empower skillful mystical adventure that isn't confined to the human plane, or through the six senses alone. It's an existential sense door: opening up to what Michio Kaku points to in his string theory, and Stephen Hawking and Buddhism and Sufism; this simultaneity of multi-dimensions, which has really become fascinating to me now that I've been di-agnosed with this fatal heart condition. It's like, "Wow, I've been catalyzed into another dimension of psychic adventure." It challenges the deep 1960's 'Be Here Now'-inspired spirituality of a privileged American being eternally present now and now and now again. What about the future? Caring for the future. Caring for the future of life. Breaking free of 'The Now' and liberating ourselves to include a radical wonderment of 'over there', beyond the known, beyond here and now; a mystical wormhole to a parallel universe that does not need Buddhism or Sufism to figure it out. A dimension beyond suffering.

And of course, it comes right back to here and now on Earth, and 'Why?' You're a father. I'm a father. You're a grandfather. I can hear my daughter, I can hear Greta, I can hear the children, I can hear your grandchildren, coming through my own fractured soul saying, "Hey guys, take the emphasis off your mystical adventure or grieving and death and dying, which is groovy, but think about the living and the about-to-be-born. What are you doing with the preciousness of your wisdom, the best years of your life, with the wisdom that you've gained? Why aren't you telling the Davosian Global Elites to call off their lies and collusion with China and a global surveillance system intended to enslave? Why aren't you doing more to preserve the future of life?" Those are some of the questions that come to me a lot when I'm taking care of my own dying process.

I don't mean to pressure you — it must be the psychedelics! [Laughing] I so wish I could get back on stage here on Maui, but you'd have to be quadruply vaxed and wear a swastika on your lapel or wear a full-body condom with an Armani label!

RBB: You're outrageous. I love it. And thank you. I too wish you'd get back on stage, and I'll come with you! [Laughing] 'A Spiritually Incorrect Night of Death, Dying and Grieving.' But back to the point. I don't feel pressured at all. I mean, they are big questions, important questions. They are questions for all of us right now, and honestly, I don't know the longer answer or the tomorrow answer. Maybe at some point we all are going to stop what we're doing and go stand somewhere and refuse to do anything until the madness stops. We may all have to do that at some point — and soon.

Now regarding the question of "Given what we know, and what you've just described, what are you going to do now?" The tricky thing here is this notion of *do, do, do, do, do*. And that's pretty much how we got into this mess in the first place! I'm thinking we had to *do* it and we had to *face it* — by *doing* something else — and then *fix it* by doing something else; and all we've done in my view is compounded the thing by thinking we have to continue to be Action People! And yes, there's time for right action, no question about it. And I wasn't saying grieving was the alternate to activity — not at all. I'm one example of someone who is carrying my grief and doing my best to love everybody and be useful and effective out here. I know it's possible. But sometimes that's an avoidance of getting into bed and staying in bed, when someone's grieving. We're around people who would just as soon not get out of bed and not go out and wish they were dead instead of their kid who just died, for example. Sooner or later these people do get out of bed, often with bigger hearts. And people are often afraid, when I sit with them, that they're going to drown in their grieving. But that doesn't happen. I don't see it.

Of course, we need our community to be around us, keep an eye and ear on us, make sure we eat and drink and get out into nature, but we don't drown. I actually find it's a place to stand on, an empowering place to stand on, because I think the unacknowledged grief is where we are culturally stuck, and we are experiencing the consequences of unacknowledged grief of countless generations before us. Grieving is often the antidote to fear, despair and powerlessness. 'Here's something we *can* do!'

AC: Let me ask a personal question: Do you sense that I am in denial of grieving?

RBB: Well, you've been in this Buddhist world for a long time, and a lot of us that got on these spiritual paths really got good at spiritual override. We decided some things just weren't spiritual. But clearly, everything has a spiritual aspect. 'Spiritual' isn't some separate luxury item. So, then, why does the world look like this? As you know, it's at the core of Buddha's teaching: Ignorance, ignorance of our true nature.

You may ask, for instance, *what* are we grieving? And I would say, "We are grieving everything that we love and care about that we have either lost or will lose. That in order to love deeply, grieving is right there, but it's often unacknowledged and pushed away." We need to stop seeing grieving as a downer.

Who wants to think, when they're in their twenties and getting married, that "*One of us is going to die, and we don't know when*"? We don't understand that that's actually a very enriching experience. When you stand in front of me and we have a conversation and we're both in awareness that either one of us could die and we don't know when, that tends to bring us fully into, "This might be the last time I talk to or see this person." How many of us have had a lousy experience of, "Oh, I wish that wasn't the last time that I spoke to that person." A lot of us have had that experience.

AC: Interesting, and thank you. The other reason I came to Maui, as mentioned earlier, was to enter hospice, go through that process, and equally, more importantly, was to make good on the State of Hawaii's 'Your Body, Your Choice Act' or the Dignity with Death Act. If deemed fit by psychologists, doctors, and nurses, you are given, as you know, the pharmaceutical compounds necessary to take your life. I have them now, in my home, anointed on a sacred altar where I have been in an alchemical dialogue with them for the past few months. It's compelling to know that you can sit there in this sacred space and within 10 minutes drink this elixir and transition to wherever the mystery takes you, based on your belief or *karma* or the current of life, or all these and much more. Who knows, really? And I go, "Wow, just mindfully sip the elixir and take your mind higher!" and so I feel like I've got an existential Rolls Royce to *Deva Dhamma* heaven, the celestial abodes.

Most people don't have that type of *Dharma* opportunity — the elegance of sacred choice to transition on your own terms. Again, as mentioned earlier, so many others are living in horror, in torturous prison camps in Burma, Syria, Iraq,

Afghanistan. They're traumatized and starving, thinking: "Who wants to live in this hell?" But I say to myself, "Alan, you've got this tropical island with gorgeous people with this incredible substance in a sacred home environment on a dying planet, with dying oceans where Greta's screaming to the world, "We don't want any more of your obsession with profit, privilege and power!" Save the world and go into high dose rehab and break the spell of your hubris and denial. The whole show appears to be coming down and now that I am 'terminal' I've been gifted with what it takes to peacefully transition, on my terms, and at any time."

RBB: How does that feel?

AC: It's both surreal and exhilarating. Probably a bit like I imagine the Metaverse on acid. Frankly, on a heart level, I feel a bit guilty that I'd be leaving behind the complexity of a dying world. My former partner and beloved friend Jeannine Davies and I talk a lot, and she's helped me contemplate what my value might be in staying alive — which may not be long, according to the medical pundits. But regardless, "Take it off *you*, Alan. There is nothing you cannot face and deal with, no matter how severe the suffering may be!" And my thoughts have moved towards "Keep on living with it, and leave it behind. Go high and Holy. Come when, I'm all in, God. Take the fear out of living and live on with a wide-open heart!" And as you said so beautifully, "Plant seeds. Do what you can for the future of life."

And then I return at times to actively designing my final three weeks before taking the sacred drink. What would those three weeks look like? A rebirthing extravaganza, so to speak. Until I come back home and ask: "What is left undone, that I could still do?" That is my essential question and one I answer and evolve daily, even multiple times in a day.

Yet, back to grieving. I'm struggling with the word because it seems to inhibit me from joyful or impassioned action. Not Action-action, but from seeing the value of living, breathing, creating, seeding the present for a better future.

On the other hand, I've been active in writing a children's' book, and releasing a World Dharma video book, as well as crafting a film, which is part spoken-word performance — a cinematic mandala that humanizes the full range of emotions, while confronting — and this is my favorite topic — the rise of global totalitarianism. It's called *'Raw War.'* I think all this may be keeping me from drinking the drink...

RBB: Grief just has a bad rap. It's that lousy marketing.

AC: Is there another word for grief, one that's more empowered?

RBB: Why do you want another word? What's another word for love? Love ain't good enough? [Smiles]

AC: I like the word 'love', but 'grief' is like sandpaper on my soul.

RBB: I hear that, I do. I also hear that coming back to your guilt around leaving a planet that needs every one of us, really. That's your koan, you know. "What is this thing, grief? And has it been with me my entire life?" And how beautiful. That's just it. We don't see grief as a beautiful thing.

AC: That's a lovely association. Now, I'm feeling into this at a more truthful level. For instance, I recently saw my beloved daughter Sahra Bella, she just turned 15. And upon departure, as beautiful as it was, I felt the poignancy of my attachment to her. Of not being able to participate in her life. And I multiply my daughter times a million others unable to participate in this thing called the miracle of existence... And so I'm hearing you now, and I'm feeling you. Thank you for the gentle reminder.

RBB: Thank you for getting there.

AC: I have a fear of attachment, that is really what that points to. And I think the fear shields me somewhat from the feeling of grief. It scares me a bit to be that vulnerable, which is not very Buddhist. Although I cry at times with laughter and joy, I can also put my head in a bucket of sorrow, so thank you for that gift. Maybe that's what we need, to have a collective cry on this planet.

RBB: I believe we do. On a regular basis. Absolutely. Wouldn't that be amazing? Let's forget all our differences for a time and just cry for the sorrows of the world.

AC: May it be so, and we could make the ninth element on the eightfold Buddhist path 'Right Crying'. The empowerment of tears or the wisdom of vulnerability. I know it's a bit cliched to use that word these days, like 'authenticity', but maybe we can dive into that in the final few minutes, the meaning of grace. There's something elegant about the word 'grace'. How to gracefully anoint the grieving with authentic actions that lead to an existential juxtaposition, where on the one hand we cry from grieving a dying planet, and on the other we joyfully act without attachment to outcome?

RBB: I don't think it's one hand or the other hand. I think it's this love-soaked grief-soaked miracle. How can we make our heart big enough to hold all the joy and at the same time all the pain of the world? And how do we stay sane and grounded in doing so? That becomes a place of refuge. That's grace. And again, we come back to, "We're going to die, and we don't know when." Sometimes that's the catalyst.

What happens when you go to a memorial or a funeral and everybody's having what I call a 'near death' experience, a 'close encounter with death'? Somebody close to us has just died, something happens to us. We can hear about people dying all over the world all the time and it's just like, "Yep." And then your best friend dies, and something happens to pretty much everybody that shakes people out of this cultural sleepwalking into something I see as a deeply spiritual experience. We step into the preciousness and fragility of life, and we immediately come to what's most important, which most often are our relationships, and we cut out the rest of the crap. This is why I like guiding funerals and memorials. Everyone is in that state.

Isn't that what a spiritual practice is for? To shake us into wakefulness here and now, and to recognize that we live inside a miracle, and now what do we want to do? And let's be willing to see the parts that are broken? So much is broken. Yes, it's all perfect, and it's broken, and we grieve about that. If you're paying attention, how could you not be upset and grieving? How do you carry that? It's what we've been talking about. How can we still dance and be joyous, play and be silly and wander on the internet, and at the same time be willing to not be in denial about what we're feeling about what is happening everywhere?

You were talking about the rest of creation; the nature of any creature is that it takes up space. We take up a certain amount of space and stuff has to get out of our way, and stuff has to die for us to have the space we need to do what we do, and to eat and to carry on; and so does every other creature. That's life and death; things have to die for us to live. How do we embrace that, as well? What a beautiful play. And I don't call it an illusion. People say death is an illusion, and I say, "Well, if death is an illusion, then everything is an illusion." And maybe everything *is* an illusion. And maybe everything is absolutely real, and the absolute and the relative are equally absolutely true. Death, no death.

Again, we come back to that great question, "OK, so now what do we do?" You asked me that and again I think grieving is a place to start. And the people that think you get stuck there, I don't see that. I think it becomes a place of empowerment for real action.

AC: It takes courage to act and grieve, as I am hearing you. Let me ask, what does courage mean to you?

RBB: Well, the immediate thing that comes to me is that you may not be fearless, but you don't let the fear get in the way of what you see needs to happen, what you need to do. We all need a tremendous amount of strength and courage at this point.

AC: In respect of the decades of your own spiritual and human development, your own practices, your own trainings, and the wisdom of your life collectively up to this moment, how would you encourage someone to foster greater courage in their life?

RBB: Don't be afraid to do what's in your heart. Ask for help from the unseen, from your ancestors, ask to have a pure intention to be of benefit. Don't care about what your parents think or what your friends think. I mean, certainly I care about what the people close to me think, but it's rare that I let it get in the way if I'm connected to an inner knowing. There's an inner knowing inside all of us. Our Sufi lineage calls it the spirit of guidance. That is where God is revealing itself to us constantly, if we listen.

How often do we honor that, and follow that guidance? We need to. If we depend on anything out here to tell us what's true and what's real, we're doomed. We've got to follow our passion and our heart and listen deeply inside. Go ahead, be amazing — and see what happens.

Regarding young people, we come back to this thing of, "What's the point? It's so big. Maybe it's too far gone, it's too late." That's why we see a lot of young people who are just like, "What the fuck? There's nothing we can do. Let's party!" and "We're powerless. It's too big." And then some of those people might come to me and say, "What do we do?" And I often say, "Find out what it is you absolutely love, where your passion is, and find out where that meets what the world needs right now. The world may be ending, plant seeds anyway."

AC: Amen. What a different world it would be if we had recited that from grade one onward. It brings me to an urgent issue: The term 'global totalitarianism' is somewhat ubiquitous, at least among those who are politically minded and attentive to freedom and universal human rights. In terms of what we have been speaking about, listening deeply to one's own heart and having the courage both to hear it and moreover, to act, abide, and be in alignment with it. Our respect for conscience compels us to have the courage to tell the truth, and the skillful courage to discern misinformation from truth. Let me ask, how do we foster the courage to be critically questioning of information and sources of misinformation? How do we tell our friends and family, and sometimes our own parents, and our children, that we don't agree with them, and yes, still love them?

Why am I bringing this up? Because the masses, as I see it, are essentially hypnotized by mass propaganda and lies. And the courage it takes to discern the truth today, and even more so, the courage to be in solidarity with the truth, has never been more important. Every one of us is called upon to answer, "What does the merger of existential rebellion and civil disobedience look like today, as an action of

non-participation in lies designed to denigrate life?"
That takes a lot of moral courage. That's the spiritual battle of our lifetime. That's why I am determined to make *'Raw War'* a final act of conscience, before my ship or the ship or both go down.

RBB: So, what I'm hearing is that you're grieving, out loud.

AC: Please, say more.

RBB: Well, if you think about where we started and what we've basically focused on this whole time, it seemed to me all of a sudden you went into a side stream.

AC: Courage, I went to courage.

RBB: Yeah, and the way it was then voiced to me looked and sounded like grieving, and it felt to me like grieving out loud.

AC: That's interesting. I don't know that it's true, but I want to have more insight to truly know the emotion that motivates this.

RBB: I wouldn't call grieving an emotion, just as I'd say love is more than an emotion.

AC: Well, what I'm saying is that it's a caring that I feel in me, and some relationship to the perception of injustice, and something to do with the love of freedom and democracy, and the collective anguish that I feel from my brothers and sisters in

Burma. I can't divorce myself from the Russian insanity in Ukraine, and Putin putting his nuclear arsenal on high alert, and in my beloved country of Burma undergoing a dystopian hell with multiple friends in prison while much of the world essentially asks: "What shall we watch on Netflix tonight?" We're 'Sleepwalking to Armageddon', as my friend Dr Helen Caldicott said in her book, titled as such. It's like, *"Fuck man!"* It brings out the Martin Luther King 'sacred rage' in me. Maybe that's grieving too. But I want to be more vocal about voicing the difficult. Is that grieving and courage mixed with hope? What would you say to that?

RBB: I'm saying I'm hearing grieving out loud. I've heard about injustice and caring and many deep conflicting feelings...

AC: But grieving here is a positive emotion.

RBB: I never said it was a negative emotion. I never even called it an emotion.

AC: What is it then, for you, please?

RBB: You acted it out. It's a humanity. It's our heart. It's our heart breaking. It's what is resonating with the truth of what's happening, and what has been happening and a willingness to not turn away. I mean, do you want me to talk about love?

It's the same thing. We could spend a long time talking about it, but you acted it out. Well, you didn't act it out; you let it take over. That's what I saw. I saw that all of a sudden you shifted into your grieving, and the way you expressed it was, "I'm grieving about those very things. And so are billions of other people."

AC: The way I feel is an innocence and a maturing of love, rather than grieving. I'm trying to express my love of existence, and it hurts.

RBB: Beautiful! Again, love and grief are twin sisters and where you find one, you'll find the other. And they can both hurt. How beautiful that we can be hurt in these ways!

AC: The courage to care about things larger than your own self-interest; it's beautiful. That is an epic note to begin the future of grieving on. May grieving go global, go viral.

RBB: Absolutely.

AC: Reverend Sir, thank you from my heart for your extraordinary expression of wisdom and grace, and grieving. May I encourage support, as we end this conversation today, for this gentleman and his miracle work with his wife and his colleagues, his allies and his friends.

RBB: Alan, you said, 'transitioned', you said 'passed', and 'passed away', but not once in an hour and a half did you say 'died'.

AC: Maybe I need to grieve that word, then. Died. As L-I-V-E-D. I am graced and honored to have shared this time and this conversation with you.

RBB: That was beautiful, thank you. I love that.

AC: When I die, thank you for taking care of my body.

RBB: If I don't die first.

AC: From my heart, thank you.

RBB: Thank you.

About Reverend Bodhi Be

"The Death Store is going to respect our new
culture where we can bring death out of the
shadows, and Bodhi is our leader. Every time you
think of dying, think of this store."
RAM DASS *(at The Death Store Grand Opening
on Maui October 2012)*

Reverend Bodhi Be
'Warrior of the heart, protector of the sacred'.

Reverend Bodhi Be is an ordained interfaith
minister and teacher in the Sufi lineage of Samuel
Lewis and Hazrat Inayat Khan. He is the founder
and executive director of Doorway Into Light, a
nonprofit organization on Maui, which provides
conscious and compassionate care for the dying,

their families, the grieving, those who work in these fields and all those 'who may die one day' and has been offering community presentations and trainings since 2006 in the fields of awakened living and dying, and the care of the dying.

Since 2012 Doorway Into Light has been operating Hawaii's only nonprofit certified green funeral home. It also operates a storefront on Maui, 'The Death Store', an educational resource center and store providing education, support and counsel on a donation basis.

A Maui resident for 45 years, he and his wife have raised 5 children and are now helping to raise 3 grandchildren. An organic, off-the-grid homesteader in Hawaii for 26 years, he grows tropical fruit with his wife, children and grandchildren.

Bodhi is a funeral director providing before- and after-death care; an end-of-life and bereavement counselor and educator; a hospice volunteer; a teacher and trainer of death doulas; a speaker and workshop leader; and a ceremonial guide. He hosts a weekly streaming radio show, 'Death Tracks', on a Maui station and on the web.

Bodhi guides memorials and funerals and leads grief rituals. He has facilitated grief support groups for teenagers at a local high school. He has trained hundreds of doctors, nurses, hospice staff, social workers, ministers, chaplains, therapists, artists and lay people in the spiritual, psychological, emotional and logistical care of the dying and the care of the dead, and for 4 years has taken dozens through a certification program to be death doulas. Bodhi has written a column called 'Ask the Death Professor' for a local Maui magazine. He is a public notary, a coffin maker and a Reiki practitioner.

Bodhi and his wife Leilah have been leading spiritual retreats in Hawaii and around the since 2007.

Bodhi is currently teaching courses through the Esalen Institute Healing Arts program in Big Sur. The 6 week course, 'We're All Gonna Die' encompasses: Cultivating a healthy relationship with our own approaching death, doing the work of preparing for death, learning skills for caring for a dying person(s) and for showing up for what's dying in the world.

For many years Bodhi collaborated with Ram Dass, a neighbor, mentor and friend, who served on Doorway Into Light's Board of Directors.

Bodhi is continuing the work Ram Dass helped birth in the fields of conscious dying in America. Doorway Into Light is currently raising funds to develop a new model of land stewardship that includes a natural green burial ground, sanctuary, park, ceremony hall and community gathering place.

IPUKA

Reverend Bodhi Be and Doorway Into Light are seeking funds and land to develop a new community model for Hawaii and the world, where life and death interweave in healthy community life. Along with a natural green burial ground where plants, gardens and trees can be planted over graves, the land will include a pet cemetery, a children's playground and art workshop, a flower farm, a community gathering place for events and a ceremony hall for memorials, funerals and other community rituals. A sanctuary of trails, ponds and benches.

The larger story includes IPUKA becoming a world-class 'dying center' that includes our training programs for conscious living, dying, and care of the dead. A place to offer psychedelic support in nature to the dying. A 'guest house' for the dying and their families where our trained death doulas provide care and companionship.

Doorway Into Light has transformed the funeral home experience from a money driven 'business' to not-for-profit sacred service and we continue to bring dying, death and the care of the dead back to 'village building' community work utilizing regenerative, inexpensive and spiritually inclusive practices.

"The Death Store is going to respect our new culture where we can bring death out of the shadows and Bodhi is our leader. Every time you think of dying, think of The Death Store."

RAM DASS

For more information, visit:

www.doorwayintolight.org
www.ipuka.org
info@doorwayintolight.org

Facebook:
Bodhi Be
The Death Store/Doorway Into Light

Facebook Group:
Doorway Into Light Ministry of Death

Instagram:
@thedeathstoremaui

Media and speaking inquiries for Rev Bodhi Be
info@doorwayintolight.org

Bodhi Be *(credit: Jon Woodhouse)*

Bodhi Be / If Found Dead *(credit: Carol Binstock)*

The Death Store (*credit:Darren Eagleheart*)

Ram Dass and Bodhi Be (*credit: Jonathan Ciser*)

Ocean Burial (*credit: Mayanna Anderson*)

Alan Clements and Bodhi Be (*credit: Doorway Into Light*)

About Alan Clements

AFTER DROPPING OUT of the
University of Virginia in his
second year, despite his scholar-
ship, Boston-born Alan Clements
went overland to India and the
East, to become one of the first
Westerners to ordain as a Buddhist monk in
Myanmar (formerly known as Burma). He lived at
the Mahasi Sasana Yeiktha (MSY) Mindfulness
Meditation Centre for nearly four years, training in
the practice and teaching of Satipatthana *Vipassana*
(Insight) meditation and Buddhist psychology
(*Abhidhamma*), under the guidance of his preceptor
the Venerable Mahasi Sayadaw and his successor,
Venerable Sayadaw U Pandita.

In 1984, forced by the dictator Ne Win to
leave the country with no reason given, Clements

returned to the West and through invitation, lectured widely on 'The Wisdom of Mindfulness' and led mindfulness-based meditation retreats and trainings throughout the US, Australia, and Canada, including assisting at a three-month Mindfulness Teacher Training with the Venerable Sayadaw U Pandita at the Insight Meditation Society (IMS), in Massachusetts.

In 1988, Alan integrated into his Buddhist training an awareness that included universal human rights, social injustice, environmental sanity, political activism, the study of propaganda and mind control in both democratic and totalitarian societies, and the preciousness of everyday freedom. His efforts working on behalf of oppressed peoples led Jack Healey, a former director of Amnesty International, to call Alan "one of the most important and compelling voices of our times."

As an investigative journalist Alan has lived in some of the most highly volatile areas of the world. In the jungles of Burma, in 1990, he was one of the first eyewitnesses to document the mass murder and oppression of ethnic minorities by Burma's military dictatorship, which resulted in his first book, 'Burma: The Next Killing Fields?' (Graced with a foreword by His Holiness the Dalai Lama).

Shortly thereafter, Alan was invited to the former Yugoslavia by Marcia Jacobs, a senior officer for the United Nations, where, based in Zagreb during the final year of the war, he wrote the film 'Burning' (for Chartoff Productions) while consulting with NGOs and the United Nations on 'The vital role of consciousness in understanding human rights, freedom, and peace'.

In 1995 a French publisher asked Alan to attempt re-entering Burma with the purpose of meeting Aung San Suu Kyi, the leader of her country's pro-democracy movement and 1991 recipient of the Nobel Peace Prize. He met with Aung San Suu Kyi, who had just been released from six years of incarceration, and invited her to share her country's courageous story with the world, together recording and illuminating the philosophical and spiritual underpinnings of Burma's nonviolent struggle for freedom, known as a 'Revolution of the Spirit'.

The transcripts of their five months of conversations were smuggled out of the country and became the book 'The Voice of Hope'. Translated into numerous languages, 'The Voice of Hope' offered insight into totalitarianism, mind control, freedom and nonviolent revolution. The London Observer reviewer stated: "Clements is the perfect interlocutor...Whatever the future of Burma, a possible future for politics itself is illuminated by these conversations."

Clements also co-authored (with the New York Times bestselling author Leslie Kean and a contributing photographer) 'Burma's Revolution of the Spirit', Aperture, NY, a large format photographic tribute to Burma's nonviolent struggle for democracy, again with a foreword by the Dalai Lama and essays by eight Nobel Peace laureates. In addition, Clements was the script revisionist and principal adviser for *Beyond Rangoon* (Castle Rock Entertainment), a feature film depicting Burma's struggle for freedom, directed by John Boorman.

In 1999 Alan founded World Dharma, a non-sectarian organization of self-styled seekers, artists, rebels, writers, scholars, journalists, and activists dedicated to a trans-religious, independent approach to personal and planetary transformation (through the integration of global human rights, meditation, and the experiential study of consciousness) with a life of expression through the arts, media, activism and service.

In 2002 Alan wrote 'Instinct for Freedom — Finding Liberation Through Living' (New World Library and World Dharma Publications), a memoir about his years in Burma which chronicles his pursuit of truth and freedom while illuminating the framework of the World Dharma vision that also forms the basis for the newly released ten-hour, 37-chapter video book, 'A Guide to the Practice of World Dharma — the *Dharma* Art of Mindful Intelligence, that of Finding Liberation Through Living'. The World Dharma Video Book is offered through Vimeo On Demand and through the World Dharma Online Institute (WDOI) that he co-founded with his colleague, Dr Jeannine Davies.

'Instinct for Freedom' was nominated for the Best Spiritual Teaching/Memoir by the National Spiritual Booksellers Association in 2003 and has been translated into numerous languages.

Alan's most recent books include: 'Wisdom for the World — The Requisites of Reconciliation: Alan Clements in Conversation with Venerable Sayadaw U Pandita of Burma'; 'Burma's Voices of Freedom: An Ongoing Struggle for Democracy' (a four volume set of books co-authored with Fergus Harlow); a spoken word album on SoundCloud titled *'Freedom: Acts of Conscience*, with music by Intext; 'Extinction X-Rated — An Auto-fictional Dark Satire On Good and Evil'; and 'A Future to Believe In — 108 Reflections on the Art and Activism of Freedom', inspired by and dedicated to his daughter Sahra Bella. The latter work has received distinguished praise from numerous leaders and activists, including Dr Helen Caldicott, Joanna Macy, Dr Vandana Shiva, Bill McKibben, Paul Hawken, and Derrick Jensen (environmental poet laureate) who wrote:

"This culture is killing the planet. If we are to have any future at all, we must unlearn everything the culture has taught us and begin to listen to the planet, to listen to life — the core intelligence of nature and the human heart. This book not only helps us with the unlearning process — the greatest challenge humankind has ever faced — it provides the essential wisdom, the spiritual intelligence, to open ourselves to finally start to hear."

In addition, Alan has presented to such organizations as Mikhail Gorbachev's State of The World Forum, The Soros Foundation, United Nations Association of San Francisco, the universities of California, Toronto, Sydney, and many others, including a keynote address at the John Ford Theater for Amnesty International's 30th year anniversary. Alan was also a presenter at the Touche Global Consciousness Conference 2019 in Bali.

Alan has been interviewed for Time and Newsweek magazines, CBC TV Canada, ABC Australia, the New York Times, Sydney Morning Herald, Radio Free Asia, Democracy Now, Talk to America, Mother Jones, Yoga Journal, The Village Voice, and scores of other print, radio and television media throughout the world.

In conjunction with the BSNO at the Mahasi Sasana Yeiktha, Yangon, Myanmar, along with their Senior Nayaka Sayadaws Alan, along with his colleagues at the Buddha Sasana Foundation of America/Canada, Dr Ingrid Jordt and Dr Jeannine Davies, conduct an annual Ten Day International Wisdom of Mindfulness Meditation Retreat for English speaking participants at Mahasi Sasana Yeiktha Yangon (MSY), Myanmar.

For more information, visit:
AlanClements.com or WorldDharma.com

To be released soon (2022): Additional books by Alan

Tonight I Met A Deva, An Angel of Love, a children's' book endorsed by the Dalai Lama, 2022

Facing Death: Alan Clements In Conversation with Reverend Bodhi Be, 2022

And a book of poetry: A satirical, irreverent and co-medic spoken word performance film, titled: *Raw War — The Spiritual Battle of Our Lifetime to Stop the Rise of Global Totalitarianism*

Media and speaking inquires for Alan Clements: contact@worlddharma.com

"*Awakening World Dharma* rests upon a basic recognition that life experience is our greatest teacher and therefore our genuine source for spiritual awakening. It is awareness that liberates, not a teacher, nor a doctrine, nor a form. "

—ALAN CLEMENTS

"How to describe Alan's presentations? A tall order. Love poems/riffs/odes/chants to the goddesses of compassion, deeply inscribed with the blood of Burmese slaves, soldiers in Iraq, Palestinian children, freedom fighters anywhere. A momentary entry into an internal tête-à-tête, ad infinitum; a glimpse at all that inner discursive dialogue which marks us unequivocally as members of the human race. Just in case we get too spiritual, let's not forget that we are required, by nature, to include everything. To paraphrase the late Vietnamese monk Thich Nhat Hahn's poem, 'Please Call Me by My True Names', I am both the 12-year-old raped girl and the pirate who raped her. It is difficult to reconcile seeming opposites, and it takes the heart of a poet. Thich Nhat Hahn is a poet; Alan is one as well."

—MARCIA JACOBS, *a psychotherapist specializing in victims of war, rape, and trauma; a senior U.N. representative for refugees in Bosnia and Croatia, 1993–1997; and a former officer of the International War Crimes Tribunal*

"Alan's life is material for a legend. An intellectual artist, freedom fighter and former Buddhist monk, he shares his insights and experience with a passion rarely seen and even more rarely lived. He'll make you think and feel in ways that challenge your entire way of being."

—CATHERINE INGRAM, *Author of In the Footsteps of Gandhi and Passionate Presence*

"I have known Alan for well over three decades. He is my first call when I seek insight and candor concerning personal and professional advice. As a speaker, his eloquence moves audiences to ask the questions behind questions about how we live, why we work, and how it fits together. Alan's presence — his remarkable ability to engage an audience and connect with their heart — stands alongside the best talent I have seen in the world."

—**ROBERT CHARTOFF**, *Producer of Rocky, The Right Stuff, and Raging Bull*

"One of the most important and compelling voices of our times... Alan Clements is a riveting communicator — challenging and inspiring. He articulates the essentials of courage and leadership in a way that can stir people from all sectors of society into action; his voice is not only a great contribution during these changeful times, it is a needed one."

—**JACK HEALEY**, *former director of Amnesty International, and founder of the Human Rights Action Center*

Also by Alan Clements

Praise for **A Future to Believe In: 108 Reflections on the Art and Activism of Freedom**

"This book is the music of wisdom, a dance with the finest places of the human heart. It is also like a walk with your favorite friends, mentors and teachers as they point out the beauties of the journey. You will want to keep this timeless treasure within reach, so you can open it to any page, and let a paragraph or a line ignite you again to the truth of your own being."

—JOANNA MACY, *Author of World as Lover, World as Self*

"Distilling the essence of world religions, cultures, politics, and spiritual traditions, Alan Clements' magnificent, timely book provides a courageous and intelligent compass personifying our aspirations for freedom and wisdom, and in so doing offers insights on how to actively shape a future that gives life hope. With our planet in peril, it is imperative that we act now to provide a secure future for our children and future generations. Make this book your guide, mentor and friend."

—DR HELEN CALDICOTT, *Author of Nuclear Power is Not the Answer and If you Love this Planet; Founding President of Physicians for Social Responsibility*

"In this radiant book is a new consciousness."

—LOWRY BURGESS, *artist, professor, creator of the first official Non-Scientific Art Payload taken into outer space by NASA in 1989*

"A Future to Believe In is a treasure, not a mere book."

—PAUL HAWKEN, *Author of Blessed Unrest*

"This transformational treasure is more relevant now than ever before, and perhaps the most important book available to face the global crisis head on and transform our lives and the planet for the better. Please join the revolution and share word of this masterpiece of 'mindful intelligence' and compassion with the world."

—MARCIA JACOBS, *Psychotherapist specializing in work with victims of war, rape and trauma. A senior staff member of the UN and other humanitarian agencies from 1993 — 2005, working with refugees and other war-traumatized populations*

"At a time when the contemporary spiritual landscape has become dangerously gentrified and domesticated, Alan Clements restores us to our senses — wild and elemental. He summons the voices of those who, alongside him, have not traded their souls for the market-driven need to be tame or acceptable, and points us to the wilderness of true, engaged, fiercely authentic awakening. This is why we are alive — to set freedom free, in ourselves and for others, in every aspect of our lives from the most mundane daily task, to the most profound political act."

—KELLY WENDORF, *Author and editor of Stories of Belonging*

"A Future to Believe In provides us with a standing wave of insight, a perpetually central pivot pertaining eminently to private and political spheres, inextricable, after all. This book should be made mandatory world-wide for all heads of state."

—LISSA WOLSAK, *Author of In Defense of Being; Squeezed Light; and Pen Chants*

"We live in times that spread greed, violence, fear and hopelessness. We live in times when consumerism enslaves us while offering pseudo-freedom. Alan Clements' labor of love, A Future to Believe In: A Guide to Revolution, Environmental Sanity, and the Universal Right to Be Free, brings us reflections that inspire us to be free and fearless."

—DR VANDANA SHIVA, *Author of Earth Democracy; Justice, Sustainability, and Peace; Soil, Not Oil; and Staying Alive*

Praise for **Instinct for Freedom: Finding Liberation Through Living**

"During an era when a spate of shallow, narcissistic fiction has found a niche as 'sacred literature' Alan's work is a wonderful relief and reminder that the heart of spirituality still is, and will always be, compassion."

—BO LOZOFF, *Founder of the Prison Ashram Project and Human Kindness Foundation and author of We're All Doing Time and It's a Meaningful Life*

"Rarely has a book touched me as deeply and personally as 'Instinct for Freedom'. This profound work is a call to action, a spiritual force for change. May the beauty of Alan's writing and the power of his personal journey compel you to be true to your own heart, so that we may all experience the gift of freedom in its purest form."

—CHERYL RICHARDSON, *Author of Stand Up for Your Life*

"This superbly written, profound, and moving work addresses head-on the central question of our time: how to put meditation into action and so transform the real conditions of the real world. Its honesty and passion are liberating, and its message both timeless and acutely timely."

—ANDREW HARVEY, *Author of The Direct Path and Sacred Activism*

"Courageous and compelling, 'Instinct for Freedom' is a vivid account of how one man's renunciation gave way to his own love and desire. This is a haunting and beautiful story, one full of teachings for seekers of all persuasions."

—MARK EPSTEIN, M.D., *Author of Going to Pieces Without Falling Apart*

Praise for **Tonight I Met A Deva, An Angel Of Love**

"This book by Alan Clements inspires people, young and old. He addresses that the reality of life can be fraught with difficulties and yet full of joy. If you have the compassion and wisdom, it's always possible to overcome whatever challenges you face. I admire Alan's determination to pass this important message onto the next generation — keeping his daughter especially in mind."

With my prayers,

THE DALAI LAMA

"Alan Clements' lovely book is pure and straight from the heart. I recommend it to every living child, to give them a true appreciation of what real life can be if the search for purity and meaning prevails."

—DR HELEN CALDICOTT, *pediatrician; founder of Physicians for Social Responsibility (Recipient of the 1985 Nobel Peace Prize)*

"This book is a gift to humanity meant to make our world a better place and to keep the future of freedom alive for generations to come. Thank you, Alan Clements. Thank you from the bottom of my heart."

—DR MA THIDA *(human rights activist, surgeon, writer, and former prisoner of conscience) is the recipient of the PEN Freedom to Write Award and the 'Disturbing the Peace' Award presented by the Vaclav Havel Foundation. She is currently on the Board of PEN International*

"Alan's book is a heart treasure. A cascade of loving radiance, rippling blessings straight into the spirit of the future, through offering a lyrical guiding Light of hope for children. May his mystical song of love invoke what it is intended to do; to serve the highest awakening of joy and beauty in us all."

—JEANNINE DAVIES, PHD, *Psychologist, Author, Relational Dharma*

"Hold on to this precious book. Read it slowly and then read it again and again and again. Keep it close. Everything you need to know is here."

—V (formerly Eve Ensler), *American playwright, performer, feminist, and activist*

"An astonishing tale from an astonishing human being: a profound poetic utterance of the spirit; a sacred offering to the vast wonders of love and beauty. Thank you, Alan Clements, for this blessing, this Dharma delight; and may the whole world bathe in its exquisite wisdom."

—LANNY CORDOVA, *Musical Artist-Activist in Afghanistan for six years and Founder and Director, The Miraculous Love Kids: Girls' Empowerment Through Music*

"This beautiful little book turns out to be a big book. Written for children—and for the inner child within all of us—this enchanting story will come as a heart-warming, soul-stirring balm for anyone who encounters it. Only a master like Clements could distill the main teachings of Buddhism into a state of such melodious, artful, poetic simplicity...And yet the book doubles as a delightfully accessible universal wisdom teaching... peering playfully into the invisible... dancing gamely with the mystical... normalizing doing so... allowing certain spiritual truths to vie for their rightful place as 'common sense'."

—NAOMI AEON, PHD., *Yale Professor turned writer, healer, and transformational teacher*

"Alan Clements has been a global bridge of wisdom and love. In this extraordinary and magical gift for children, he holds the hands of their heart while walking them across to the ancient teachings of the Buddha. As a deeply devoted father, he finds the language that can awaken their precious curiosity. It is my honor to encourage all parents to bring their children to the endearment of Alan's wise soul shared in this book."

—MITCH DAVIDOWITZ, M.S.W., M.ED., *Psychotherapist, Global Writer and Educator*

"A spectacular work of wisdom art; a magical mystery tour of beauty, purity and inspiration. I have rarely been so touched by so few words that can be carried in my heart for a lifetime. I only wish I'd had this book of celestial splendor when I was growing up. Parents, buy this mystical tale of love and wonderment and be transformed, together with your entire family."

—BROCK NOYES, *Author of Somatic Zen*

"This beautiful book, full of love and wisdom, is a worthy tribute to a life well lived and to life itself."

—DERRICK JENSEN, *Poet Laureate, Activist, Author of A Language Older Than Words*

"Alan has crafted a magical tale of wisdom and beauty that will not only touch the hearts of children, but of every adult that turns its pages as well."
—CHERYL RICHARDSON, *New York Times bestselling author of Take Time for Your Life*

"Alan Clements' book about meeting an Angel of Love is a most wondrous story, perfect to open up children's hearts and excite their curiosity. We all want to meet 'an Angel of Love' and the teachings about awakening are for every age, at any time. The sooner we open up to our infinite spiritual potential, the better. I recommend this great book. Do yourself a favor and offer it to members of your family, young and old!"
—MARGOT ANAND, *Author of The Art of Everyday Ecstasy, and more*

"'This precious book by Alan Clements is a ray of light, a transcendent story of love, hope and what some might call magic, that will uplift and inspire all who read it."
—LYNN HENDEE, *Producer of The Glorias; The Tempest; and Ender's Game*

"To understand the true nature of life, all one has to do is take this exquisite journey of the Four Noble Truths, told by Alan Clements in the most lovely, poetic way. Perhaps this is exactly what the Buddha had in mind for us to understand divine illumination through the pureness of a child's heart."
—ORA NADRICH, *Author of Mindfulness and Mysticism*

"'Tonight I Met a Deva, an Angel of Love' is a truly exquisite and luminous offering inspired by a father's love for his beloved daughter, and in particular, all young people. In this beautifully crafted rhyming fable, Alan Clements illuminates profound and complex Buddhist insights by poetically simplifying them in a way that deeply touches and opens the heart. Don't hesitate to get copies of this Dharma treasure to share, not only with the children in your life but also with friends, family and community. In our troubled times, Alan's book is like pure nectar reminding us of the divine and the very best of our humanity."
—KITTISARO & THANISSARA, *Authors of Listening to the Heart and founders of Dharmagiri (a Buddhist*

inspired retreat center in South Africa) and Sacred Mountain Sangha, California, are meditation teachers who trained as monastics, for 15 and 12 years respectively, in the Thai Forest Tradition of Ajahn Chah

"There is a visual and audible beauty in Alan's short book, 'Tonight I Met A Deva', that spoke through my child's voice as I read it. You can't help but feel the ancient wisdom flowing through those words. I think it will awaken your inner child, as it did mine — and as I believe it will for the younger innocents around us."

—JEFF KUHN, *Professor of Physics and Astronomy, University of Hawaii and Institute for Astronomy*

"For thousands of years, teachings about the inner wisdom have been transmitted through stories, myths, fairy tales, mantras, tantras, and sutras. Stories are wonderful because they bring the Dharma alive, and this enchanting book by Alan Clements, a former Buddhist monk in Burma, is a Dharma teaching in the form of a mystical story. 'Tonight I Met A Deva, An Angel of Love' comes from a daring explorer of the inner world who has had many adventures and faced many obstacles, and through it all remains a courageous and creative voice for freedom, inner and outer. I wholeheartedly recommend to parents worldwide, gift you and your beloved family with this timeless Gem of a book, and bring the Dharma home, and a higher love into the heart."

—LORIN ROCHE, *Meditation Teacher, Author of The Radiance Sutras*

"I admire the purity Alan Clements shares in his deeply moving new book, 'Tonight I Met A Deva, An Angel of Love' where he poetically illuminates the essence of the Buddha's Four Noble Truths, and done so skillfully, in a nonsectarian, nonreligious, uplifting human way. This precious work of art is especially important during these challenging times, both for our beloved children and adults as well. On a personal note, Alan graciously accepted our invitation on two occasions to speak with the students at our Sunrise School in Bali. It was an honor to have him with us, inspiring the children and answering their questions with gentleness and compassion, and also a sense of humor. He clearly touched something special in them, planting seeds of curiosity and wonderment, and that ever so rare quality of mysticism. He also offered guidance about the natural intelligence of the human heart. At the school, we are all grateful for Alan's visits. May this treasure of a book find its way into homes and classrooms around the world. And meanwhile we, the staff, teachers and students, hold you Alan, and your beloved daughter, Bella, and all Beings in our Prayers."

—SUSANNE SCHATTIN ROZIADI, *Co-founder of Sunrise School, Bali, Indonesia*

"A heartfelt love letter, a prayer for understanding, and a profound message for his daughter, Sahra Bella Clements Earl and all children, condensed into a luminous poem, 'Tonight I Met a Deva', carries Alan Clements' life-long quest: that humanity will see through the veils that cause suffering, and commence the journey for the liberation of all beings. Alan, dear treasured friend, your book is a blessing!"

—NGOC-TRAN PHAM, *singer, Teacher of voice, healing, yoga and meditation*